The Future of Work:
Identifying and Preparing for
Emerging Careers

Emmanuel Kayode Ogunyinka, Ph.D., PMP, PSM I

Tayo Akinsipe, PHR, SHRM-CP, PSM I

Edited By: Damilola James Owoeye

Cover Design By: Jonidam Graphics

Printed in the United States of America

ISBN: 979-8-3916-4388-3

For further inquiries, contact the author: ekogunyinka@itcutech.com

This book is printed on acid-free paper.

Table of Contents

About the Book

This book delivers practical guidance on anticipating and adapting to change and cultivating the essential skills and knowledge required to remain competitive in the job market. It begins by examining the principal trends shaping the future of work, such as the widespread adoption of artificial intelligence and automation and the emergence of new industries and occupations. The book then supplies practical advice on researching industry trends and analyzing job growth data to pinpoint burgeoning careers.

Additionally, the book underscores the significance of networking and seeking mentors in developing fields while emphasizing the importance of staying informed about industry news and events. It also provides recommendations on acquiring the necessary education and skills and gaining experience through internships and entry-level positions.

The book features a comprehensive collection of interview questions and answers, encompassing IT, behavioral, technical, motivational, and situational categories. It also includes suggested questions to pose to the interviewer, tips for navigating virtual job interviews, and insights into the inquiries that recruiters typically raise during telephone interviews.

In conclusion, The Future of Work: Identifying and Preparing for Emerging Careers is an indispensable resource for those seeking to excel in the rapidly evolving job market of the 21st century.

Chapter ONE

Future of Work Introduction

According to the World Economic Forum, "emerging careers" are defined as "new or recently-developed occupations that are expected to be in high demand over the coming years" (2020). These careers often arise due to technological advancements and changes in the job market. The Organization for Economic Co-operation and Development (OECD) suggests that emerging careers often involve a high level of digital literacy and the ability to adapt to rapidly changing technology (2017). These skills are becoming increasingly important in a world where automation and artificial intelligence are transforming work. According to Forbes, emerging careers are often found in industries "on the cusp of rapid growth and innovation" (2019). Examples of these industries include renewable energy, biotechnology, and digital marketing. Individuals must stay informed about emerging careers to remain competitive in the job market. The European Union's Digital Single Market Team advises individuals to "constantly update their knowledge and skills" to seize emerging career opportunities (2019).

1.1. Importance of Staying ahead of the curve in the Job Market

Staying ahead of the curve in the job market is essential for several reasons. According to the McKinsey Global Institute, the rapid pace of technological change and increasing global competition are transforming the nature of work, leading to the "rise of new roles and the decline of others" (2017). Individuals must continuously update their skills and knowledge to stay relevant and competitive in this changing job market. The World Economic Forum's "Future of Jobs Report 2020" found that over half of all employees will need significant retraining to stay employable in the next five years (2020). This highlights the importance of staying ahead of the curve and anticipating the skills in demand. The Congressional Research Service suggests that staying ahead of the curve can also involve proactively seeking new opportunities and being open to pivoting into emerging fields (2018). By being proactive and adaptable, individuals can position themselves for success in the face of constantly changing job market dynamics.

1.2. The Role of Technology in Shaping the Future of Work

Advancements in Artificial Intelligence and Automation

Artificial intelligence (AI) and automation are transforming how we work and are expected to significantly impact the job market in the coming years. According to the International Labor Organization, the proliferation of AI and automation will lead to both the displacement of some jobs and the creation of new ones (2019). AI, in particular, has the potential to revolutionize a wide range of industries by automating tasks and making them more efficient. For example, the use of AI in customer service and support roles has already led to the creation of new job roles, such as AI trainers and data analysts (McKinsey Global Institute, 2017). However, the rise of AI and automation also presents challenges for workers. The Oxford Martin School warns that certain occupations, such as those involving routine tasks, are at higher risk of being automated in the future (2014). Therefore, individuals must anticipate the potential impact of AI and automation on their industry and proactively seek opportunities to upskill and stay competitive.

1.3. **Impact on Traditional Job Industries and Creation of New Ones**

The advancement of technology, particularly artificial intelligence, and automation, is having a significant impact on traditional job industries and leading to the creation of new ones. According to the World Economic Forum, the rise of AI and automation leads to the "rise of new roles and the decline of others" (2020). Some industries, such as manufacturing and retail, are at higher risk of job displacement due to automation. In contrast, others, such as healthcare and education, are expected to see an increase in demand for skilled workers (McKinsey Global Institute, 2017). At the same time, the proliferation of technology is also leading to the emergence of entirely new industries. The OECD notes that the growth of the gig economy and the increasing demand for digital services are creating new job opportunities in fields such as online tutoring and ecommerce (2017). It is essential for individuals to stay informed about the impact of technology on their industry and to proactively seek out opportunities to upskill and adapt to these changes.

Chapter TWO

Identifying Emerging Careers

Objectives

1. Researching industry trends and analyzing data on job growth
2. Networking and seeking out mentors in emerging fields
3. Keeping up with industry news and events

2.1. Researching industry trends and analyzing data on job growth

Researching industry trends and analyzing data on job growth is essential in identifying emerging careers. By staying informed about the latest developments in your industry and understanding the factors driving job growth, you can position yourself for success in the job market. Many resources are available for researching industry trends and job growth. The World Bank's "The Future of Jobs: The Future of Work in the 21st Century" report provides data on the industries and occupations expected to grow most in the coming years (2015). Additionally, the McKinsey Global Institute's "Preparing for the Future of

Work" report offers insights into the skills that will be in demand (2017). Other valuable resources for researching industry trends are trade publications and news sites. These sources can provide valuable insights into the latest developments in your field and help you stay informed about the direction of your industry. It is also essential to be proactive in seeking out data on job growth in your field. The Congressional Research Service suggests that individuals can use government data sources like the Bureau of Labor Statistics to identify industries and occupations experiencing job growth (2018).

2.2. Networking and Seeking out Mentors in Emerging Fields

Networking and seeking mentors in emerging fields are essential in preparing for an emerging career. Building relationships with individuals already established in your field can provide valuable insights and guidance as you navigate your career. According to the Harvard Business Review, networking can help you access opportunities that may not be advertised and provide valuable introductions to potential employers or clients (2018). It is, therefore, essential to be proactive in building your network and seeking out opportunities to connect with individuals in your field. Seeking mentors is also necessary for building your network and advancing your career. A mentor can provide valuable guidance and support as you navigate your career and help you better understand the industry and the skills in demand. There are several ways to find mentors in emerging fields. The Forbes "Emerging Careers in the Digital Age" article suggests contacting industry professionals through professional associations or attending industry events and conferences (2019). LinkedIn is also valuable for finding and connecting with potential mentors in your field.

2.3. Keeping Up with Industry News and Events

Keeping up with industry news and events is essential to stay informed about emerging careers and to stay competitive in the job market. By staying current on the latest developments in your field, you can gain valuable insights into your industry's direction and the skills in demand. There are several ways to stay informed about industry news and events. Trade publications and industry news sites are valuable sources of information on the latest developments in your field. Many professional associations and organizations also host events and conferences that provide an opportunity to learn about industry trends and connect with other professionals. Attending industry events and conferences can also be a valuable way to network and connect with others in your field. The World Economic Forum's "The Future of Jobs Report 2020" suggests that individuals should "actively seek out opportunities to learn, network, and stay current" to stay competitive in the job market (2020). It is also essential to proactively seek information on industry trends and developments. The Organisation for Economic Co-operation and Development advises individuals to "constantly update their knowledge and skills" to stay current and take advantage of emerging career opportunities (2017).

Chapter THREE

Preparing For an Emerging Career

Objectives

1. Acquiring the necessary education and skills
2. Gaining experience through internships and entry-level positions
3. Continuously learning and adapting to new developments in the field

3.1. Acquiring the Necessary Education and Skills

Acquiring the necessary education and skills is essential in preparing for an emerging career. Having the knowledge and skills in demand in your field is vital. The McKinsey Global Institute suggests that individuals should "invest in lifelong learning" to stay current and adapt to the changing nature of work (2017). This may involve pursuing additional education, such as a degree or certification, or ongoing professional development to update your skills. It is also essential to be proactive in seeking opportunities to gain experience in your field. The Fast Company article

"How to Pivot into an Emerging Career" suggests internships, entry-level positions, and volunteer work to gain experience and build your skillset (2016). In addition to formal education and experience, the World Economic Forum's "The Future of Jobs Report 2020" emphasizes the importance of soft skills, such as problem-solving and critical thinking, in preparing for an emerging career (2020). Developing these skills can help you stand out in the job market and be more adaptable to changing job requirements.

3.2. Gaining Experience through Internships and Entry-Level Positions

Gaining experience through internships and entry-level positions is essential in preparing for an emerging career. These types of opportunities can provide valuable hands-on experience and allow you to better understand the industry and the skills in demand. According to the Fast Company article "How to Pivot into an Emerging Career," internships and entry-level positions can be an effective way to "test the waters" in a new field and gain experience that can be leveraged in future job searches (2016). These opportunities can also provide valuable networking opportunities and may lead to more advanced positions. The Organization for Economic Co-operation and Development advises that individuals should be proactive in seeking opportunities to gain experience in their field, whether through internships, entry-level positions, or volunteer work (2017). Knowledge can build your skillset and increase your competitiveness in the job market.

3.3. Continuously Learning and Adapting to New Developments in the Field

Continuously learning and adapting to new developments in your field is essential to preparing for an emerging career. In a rapidly changing job market, staying current and adapting to new products is necessary to remain competitive. The McKinsey Global Institute suggests that individuals should "invest in lifelong learning" to stay current and adapt to the changing nature of work (2017). This may involve pursuing additional education, such as a degree or certification, or ongoing professional development to update your skills. The World Economic Forum's "The Future of Jobs Report 2020" emphasizes the importance of continuous learning in rapid technological change (2020). To stay competitive in the job market, individuals should proactively seek opportunities to learn and adapt to new developments in their field. The Organization for Economic Co-operation and Development advises individuals to "constantly update their knowledge and skills" to stay current and take advantage of emerging career opportunities (2017). You can position yourself for success in an increasingly competitive job market by continuously learning and adapting to new developments in your field.

Chapter FOUR

Information Technology (IT) Careers

Information Technology (IT) is a rapidly growing field encompassing various careers, from software development and systems administration to network engineering and cybersecurity. In today's increasingly digital world, IT professionals play a vital role in the success of organizations by designing, building, and maintaining the technology systems that power businesses and organizations of all types and sizes. According to the US Bureau of Labor Statistics, computer and information technology employment is projected to grow 11 percent from 2019 to 2029, much faster than the average for all occupations.

IT careers offer diverse options, with varying levels of education and experience required. Some positions, such as software developer or systems administrator, may require a bachelor's degree in computer science or a related field. In contrast, others, such as network administrators or IT support specialists, may require only an associate degree or a specialized certification. Regardless of the specific career path, IT professionals are in high demand, with many offering competitive salaries and strong job security. The field of IT is also notable for being dynamic and constantly evolving, with new technologies, trends, and innovations being introduced regularly. This means those working in IT should be willing to adapt and learn new skills to remain current. The following are the trending IT careers:

4.1. **Human Resource Information Systems Analysts** (HRIS) are responsible for designing, implementing, and maintaining an organization's human resource information system. These systems are designed to manage and automate various HR functions, such as employee data management, payroll and benefits administration, and compliance with legal requirements. As

the field of HR is constantly evolving, HRIS analysts must stay current with new technologies and trends to improve and streamline HR processes. In addition, HRIS analysts must have strong communication and problem-solving skills to effectively work with technical and non-technical stakeholders and multiple teams and departments within an organization. A career as an HRIS analyst can be a challenging and rewarding opportunity for individuals who are interested in human resources and have the right combination of technical and people skills.

Degrees and certifications required: To become an HRIS Analyst, one typically needs a Bachelor's degree in Information Technology, Human Resources, or a related field. Some companies may require a Master's degree or specialized certifications in HRIS technologies or data analytics. Some of the popular HRIS certifications for HR professionals are Senior Professional in Human Resources (SPHR), Human Resource Information Professional (HRIP), Certified Professional in Learning and Performance (CPLP), Certified Compensation Professional (CCP), and Global Professional in Human Resources (GPHR).

Job growth projections: According to the Bureau of Labor Statistics (BLS), the employment of computer and information systems managers, including HRIS analysts, is projected to grow by 10 percent from 2020 to 2030, faster than the average for all occupations. The increasing demand for computer systems analysts and the growing use of technology in HR management drives the growth in this field.

Advancement opportunities: HRIS analysts can advance their careers by becoming HRIS managers, leading HR technology teams, or moving into higher-level HR management positions. They can also specialize in specific areas of HRIS, such as data analysis or software development. Advanced degrees and certifications can also enhance an HRIS analyst's career prospects. HRIS analysts can work in various industries, including healthcare, finance, and government agencies. They play a crucial role in supporting HR departments in achieving their organizational goals by streamlining HR processes and maximizing the use of technology.

4.2. **Information Technology (IT) Auditor**

reviews and assesses an organization's information systems, practices, and operations to ensure industry standards and regulations compliance. This includes assessing internal controls' effectiveness, evaluating systems and networks' security, and identifying areas for improvement. To be successful in this role, IT auditors should have a strong understanding of information systems, networks, and cybersecurity, as well as knowledge of relevant laws, regulations, and industry standards. In addition, IT auditors should have strong analytical and problem-solving skills and the ability to communicate effectively with technical and non-technical stakeholders. An IT auditor role can be an excellent career opportunity for those interested in technology with strong attention to detail, an aptitude for data analysis, and a desire to understand the business impact of technology and regulatory compliance requirements.

Degrees and certifications required: To become an IT auditor, a bachelor's degree in information technology, computer science, or a related field is typically required. Many employers prefer hiring IT auditors with a master's degree in a relevant field. Additionally, certifications such as Certified Information Systems Auditor (CISA), Certified Information Security Manager (CISM), and Certified in the Governance of Enterprise IT (CGEIT) can be beneficial for IT auditors looking to advance their careers.

Job growth projections: The demand for IT auditors is expected to grow in the coming years as organizations increasingly rely on technology to store, process, and transmit sensitive information. According to the Bureau of Labor Statistics (BLS), the employment of computer and information systems managers, which includes IT auditors, is projected to grow 10 percent from 2019 to 2029, faster than the average for all occupations.

Advancement opportunities: IT auditors can advance their careers by acquiring additional certifications and taking on more organizational responsibilities. With experience and expertise, IT auditors can move into management roles, such as IT audit manager or chief information security officer (CISO). They may also move into related fields, such as information security or cyber-risk management, where they can specialize in specific areas of IT security and risk management.

4.3. **Site Reliability Engineer (SRE)** is a type of systems administrator responsible for ensuring the reliability, scalability, and performance of an organization's systems and services. This typically includes monitoring and troubleshooting systems, automating processes and deployment, and designing and implementing improvements to systems and infrastructure. With the increasing demand for reliability and scalability in modern

techniques, the role of SREs is becoming more and more critical for the success of organizations. To succeed as an SRE, an individual must have a strong understanding of systems administration and experience with automation tools, programming languages, and infrastructure as code. In addition, SREs should have strong problem-solving skills and a focus on continuous improvement and automation. A career as an SRE can be an excellent opportunity for individuals interested in technology and system administration and looking for a challenging and rewarding career.

Degrees and certifications required: SREs typically have a bachelor's or master's degree in computer science, information technology, or a related field. Many employers prefer to hire SREs with a strong understanding of computer systems and programming languages and experience with cloud computing and network security. In addition, certifications such as Certified Information Systems Security Professional (CISSP) and Certified Cloud Security Professional (CCSP) can benefit SREs looking to advance their careers.

Job growth projections: The demand for SREs are expected to grow in the coming years as organizations increasingly rely on technology to run their businesses.

According to the Bureau of Labor Statistics (BLS), the employment of computer and information systems managers, which includes SREs, is projected to grow 10 percent from 2019 to 2029, faster than the average for all occupations.

Advancement opportunities: SREs can advance their careers by acquiring additional certifications and taking on more organizational responsibilities. With experience and expertise, SREs can move into management roles, such as IT operations manager or infrastructure manager. They may also move into related fields, such as cloud computing or DevOps, where they can specialize in specific areas of technology infrastructure and software delivery.

4.4. **Information Systems Security Manager (ISSM)** ensures the security of an organization's information systems and networks. This includes implementing and managing security protocols, monitoring systems for security breaches, and conducting security assessments and audits. To succeed as an ISSM, an individual should have a strong understanding of information systems and networks and knowledge of security best practices, regulatory compliance, and industry

standards. In addition, ISSM should have strong problem-solving, analytical, and communication skills. Information systems security management is a critical and rapidly growing field. With the increasing importance of protecting sensitive data and the growing threat of cyber-attacks, the role of ISSM is becoming more and more vital for the success of organizations. A career as an ISSM can be a challenging and rewarding opportunity for individuals passionate about technology, security, and risk management.

Information Systems Security Managers (ISSMs) are responsible for ensuring the security of a company's information systems and protecting sensitive data and assets from cyber threats. They are crucial in developing and implementing security policies, procedures, and controls to secure an organization's information technology (IT) systems and data.

Degrees and certifications required: ISSMs typically have a bachelor's or master's degree in computer science, information technology, or a related field. Many employers prefer to hire ISSMs who have experience with network security, data privacy, and cyber security. In addition, certifications such as Certified Information Systems Security Professional (CISSP), Certified in the

Governance of Enterprise IT (CGEIT), and Certified Information Security Manager (CISM) can be beneficial for ISSMs looking to advance their careers.

Job growth projections: The demand for ISSMs is expected to grow in the coming years as organizations increasingly rely on technology to store, process, and transmit sensitive information. According to the Bureau of Labor Statistics (BLS), the employment of computer and information systems managers, which includes ISSMs, is projected to grow 16 percent from 2021 to 2031, faster than the average for all occupations.

Advancement opportunities: ISSMs can advance their careers by acquiring additional certifications and taking on more organizational responsibilities. With experience and expertise, ISSMs can move into executive roles, such as chief information security officer (CISO) or chief technology officer (CTO). They may also move into related fields, such as information security or cyber-risk management, where they can specialize in specific areas of IT security and risk management.

4.5. **Network/Cloud Engineer** is responsible for designing, implementing, and maintaining an organization's network and cloud infrastructure. This includes configuring and managing routers, switches, and other networking equipment, as well as cloud infrastructure such as Amazon Web Services (AWS) or Microsoft Azure. To succeed as a Network/Cloud Engineer, an individual must have a strong understanding of networking concepts, protocols, and technologies and knowledge of cloud platforms and services, such as AWS or Azure. In addition, Network/Cloud Engineers should have strong problem-solving skills and the ability to work well in a team environment. As businesses continue to rely more heavily on cloud computing and the Internet of A Things, the role of Network/Cloud Engineers has become increasingly important. A career as a Network/Cloud Engineer can be a challenging and rewarding opportunity for individuals interested in technology and passionate about designing and maintaining networks and cloud infrastructure.

Degrees and certifications required: Network/Cloud Engineers typically have a bachelor's or master's degree in computer science, information technology, or a related field. Many employers prefer to hire Network/Cloud Engineers who have experience with network design, cloud computing, and security. In addition, certifications such as Cisco Certified Network Associate (CCNA), Amazon Web Services (AWS) Certified

Solutions Architect, and Azure Solutions Architect Expert can benefit Network/Cloud Engineers looking to advance their careers.

Job growth projections: The demand for Network/Cloud Engineers is expected to grow in the coming years as organizations increasingly adopt cloud computing and virtualization technologies. According to the Bureau of Labor Statistics (BLS), the employment of computer network architects, which includes Network/Cloud Engineers, is projected to grow 5 percent from 2019 to 2029, faster than the average for all occupations.

Advancement opportunities: Network/Cloud Engineers can advance their careers by acquiring additional certifications and taking on more organizational responsibilities. With experience and expertise, Network/Cloud Engineers can move into management roles, such as network/cloud manager or IT infrastructure manager. They may also move into related fields, such as cloud computing or network security, where they can specialize in specific areas of network and cloud infrastructure design and implementation.

4.6. **The Applications Architect** role is crucial for the organization's success in software development. An applications Architect is a technical leader responsible for designing and overseeing the development of software applications within an organization. This includes designing and developing application architecture, evaluating and selecting technology platforms, and ensuring that applications meet business and technical requirements. To be successful as an Applications Architect, an individual should have a strong understanding of software development principles and experience with various programming languages and technologies. Additionally, Applications Architects should have strong problem-solving skills, be able to lead and mentor teams and have good communication skills to work with stakeholders to understand their requirements. As technology continues to evolve, the role of an Applications Architect will continue to grow in importance, providing opportunities for career growth and advancement.

Degrees and certifications required: Applications Architects typically have a bachelor's or master's degree in computer science, software engineering, or a related field. Many employers prefer to hire application architects with experience in software development, system architecture, and project management. In addition, certifications such as Certified Solutions Architect - Associate, Azure Solutions Architect, and Oracle Certified Master, Java Enterprise Architect can benefit applications architects looking to advance their careers.

Job growth projections: The demand for Applications Architects is expected to grow in the coming years as organizations increasingly rely on software applications to run their businesses. According to the Bureau of Labor Statistics (BLS), software developers' employment, including Applications Architects, is projected to grow 21 percent from 2019 to 2029, much faster than the average for all occupations.

Advancement opportunities: Applications Architects can advance their careers by taking on more organizational responsibilities, such as leading software development projects or mentoring junior developers. With experience and expertise, Applications Architects can move into management roles, such as software development manager or IT director. They may also move into related fields, such as software architecture or systems integration, where they can specialize in specific software development and systems architecture.

4.7. **Data Architect** is responsible for designing, implementing, and maintaining an organization's data architecture. This includes tasks such as designing and maintaining data models, data integration, and data governance, as well as evaluating and selecting data management technologies. To succeed as a Data Architect, an individual should have a strong understanding of data modeling, data management, and data governance concepts and experience working with various data management technologies. Additionally, Data Architects should have strong analytical and problem-solving skills, work well in a team environment, and have good communication skills to work with stakeholders and explain complex technical concepts in simple terms. Data has become a critical business asset; therefore, the role of a Data Architect is more crucial than ever. With the increasing need for data-driven decision-making and the growing volume, variety, and velocity of data, the role of Data Architects is becoming more critical for the success of organizations. A career as a Data Architect can be a challenging and rewarding opportunity for individuals interested in data management and passionate about designing and implementing data architecture.

Data Architects are responsible for designing and maintaining an organization's data systems, ensuring they meet the business needs and are optimized for performance, scalability, and security. They play a crucial role in ensuring the accuracy and consistency of a company's data and its ability to be used for decision-making and other critical business processes.

Degrees and certifications required: Data Architects typically have a bachelor's or master's degree in computer science, information technology, or a related field. Many employers prefer to hire Data Architects who have experience with database design, data modeling, and big data technologies. In addition, certifications such as Certified Data Management Professional (CDMP), Certified Big Data Professional (CBD), and Amazon Web Services (AWS) Certified Big Data - Specialty can be beneficial for Data Architects looking to advance their careers.

Job growth projections: The demand for Data Architects is expected to grow in the coming years as organizations increasingly rely on data for decision-making and critical business processes. According to the Bureau of Labor Statistics (BLS), the employment of database administrators, which includes Data Architects, is projected to grow 11 percent from 2019 to 2029, faster than the average for all occupations.

Advancement opportunities: Data Architects can advance their careers by taking on more organizational responsibilities, such as leading data management projects or mentoring junior data analysts. With experience and expertise, Data Architects can move into management roles, such as data management manager or chief data officer. They may also move into related fields, such as data analytics or big data, where they can specialize in specific data management and analysis areas.

4.8. ***Database Administrator (DBA)*** is responsible for designing, implementing, maintaining, and administering an organization's databases. This includes ensuring the integrity and security of the data, optimizing database performance, and troubleshooting and resolving issues. DBAs also play a critical role in database systems development, testing, and deployment. To be successful as a DBA, an individual should have a strong understanding of database management systems and related technologies and experience with database design and optimization. They should also have a good knowledge of security, backup, and disaster recovery techniques and have strong analytical and troubleshooting skills. As businesses rely on data-driven decision-making and technology continues to evolve, the demand for DBAs with the skills to manage, maintain and analyze data will continue to grow. A Database Administrator role is vital for an organization's smooth running and data integrity. A career as a DBA can be a challenging and rewarding opportunity for individuals interested in data management and technology and with solid attention to detail.

Database Administrators (DBAs) are responsible for maintaining, performing, and securing an organization's databases. They are crucial in ensuring a company's data's availability, reliability, consistency, and ability for decision-making and other critical business processes.

Degrees and certifications required: Database Administrators typically have a bachelor's or master's degree in computer science, information technology, or a related field. Many employers prefer to hire DBAs who have experience with database management, data modeling, and SQL. In addition, certifications such as Oracle Certified Professional, Azure Database Administrator Associate, and Amazon Web Services (AWS) Certified Database - Specialty can benefit DBAs looking to advance their careers.

Job growth projections: The demand for Database Administrators is expected to grow in the coming years as organizations increasingly rely on databases for decision-making and critical business processes. According to the Bureau of Labor Statistics (BLS), the employment of database administrators, which includes DBAs, is projected to grow 11 percent from 2019 to 2029, faster than the average for all occupations.

Advancement opportunities: Database Administrators can advance their careers by taking on more responsibilities within their organizations, such as leading database management projects or mentoring junior database administrators. With experience and expertise, DBAs can move into management roles, such as database management manager or chief data officer. They may also move into related fields, such as data analytics or cloud computing, where they can specialize in specific data management and technology areas.

4.9. **Data Security Analyst** is responsible for ensuring the security of an organization's data by identifying, assessing, and mitigating data security risks. This includes implementing and maintaining security protocols, monitoring systems for security breaches,

performing security assessments and audits, and providing recommendations for security improvements. To succeed as a Data Security Analyst, an individual should have a strong understanding of data security concepts and technologies and experience with data security best practices, regulatory compliance, and industry standards. Additionally, Data Security Analysts should have strong analytical and problem-solving skills, work well in a team environment, and have good communication skills to work with stakeholders and explain complex technical concepts in simple terms. With the increasing importance of protecting sensitive data and the growing threat of cyber-attacks, the role of a Data Security Analyst is becoming more and more vital for the success of organizations. A career as a Data Security Analyst can be a challenging and rewarding opportunity for individuals interested in data security and risk management.

Data Security Analysts ensure an organization's data's confidentiality, integrity, and availability. They protect an organization's sensitive information and reputation by identifying, preventing, and mitigating data security risks.

Degrees and certifications required: Data Security Analysts typically have a bachelor's or master's degree in computer science, information technology, cybersecurity, or a related field. Many employers prefer to hire Data Security Analysts who have experience with network and data security, as well as certifications such as Certified Information Systems Security Professional (CISSP), Certified Ethical Hacker (CEH), and CompTIA Security+.

Job growth projections: The demand for Data Security Analysts are expected to grow in the coming years as organizations increasingly recognize the importance of data security for protecting their sensitive information and reputation. According to the Bureau of Labor Statistics (BLS), the employment of information security analysts, which includes Data Security Analysts, is projected to grow 32 percent from 2019 to 2029, much faster than the average for all occupations.

Advancement opportunities: Data Security Analysts can advance their careers by taking on more organizational responsibilities, such as leading projects or mentoring junior security analysts. With experience and expertise, Data Security Analysts can move into management roles, such as information security manager or chief information security officer. They may also move into related fields, such as cloud security or risk management, where they can specialize in specific data and information security areas.

4.10. **Big Data** is rapidly growing and becoming increasingly important for organizations seeking insights from large and varied data sets. Big Data Engineer is responsible for designing and implementing the infrastructure for large data sets, commonly called "big data." This includes designing and building data pipelines, integrating data from various sources, and optimizing data storage and retrieval. To be successful as a Big Data Engineer, an individual should have a strong understanding of big data technologies, such as Hadoop, Spark, and Kafka, as well as experience with programming languages, such as Java, Python, and Scala. Additionally, Big Data Engineers should have strong analytical, problem-solving, and troubleshooting skills, the ability to work well in a team environment, and good communication skills to work with stakeholders and explain complex technical concepts in simple terms. A career as a Big Data Engineer can be a challenging and rewarding opportunity for individuals interested in technology and passionate about working with large amounts of data.

Big Data refers to the large volume of structured and unstructured data generated from various sources, such as social media, mobile devices, and sensors, that can be analyzed to uncover insights and drive better decision-making. It is a growing field that requires combining technical and business skills to manage, analyze, and derive value from large datasets.

Degrees and certifications required: Many professionals working in Big Data have a bachelor's or master's degree in computer science, information technology, statistics, or a related field. Additionally, certifications such as Cloudera Certified Associate (CCA), Hortonworks Certified Apache Hadoop Administrator (CHA), and MapR Certified Hadoop Developer (MCHD) can be beneficial for individuals looking to demonstrate their expertise in Big Data technologies.

Job growth projections: The demand for professionals with Big Data skills is expected to grow in the coming years as organizations increasingly recognize the value of data-driven decision-making. According to the Bureau of Labor Statistics (BLS), the employment of computer and information research scientists, which includes Big Data experts, is projected to grow 16 percent from 2019 to 2029, faster than the average for all occupations.

Advancement opportunities: Big Data professionals can advance their careers by taking on more organizational responsibilities, such as leading data analytics projects or mentoring junior data scientists. With experience and expertise, they can move into management roles, such as data analytics manager or chief data officer. They may also move into related fields, such as artificial intelligence or machine learning, where they can specialize in specific data analysis and technology areas.

4.11. **Data Scientist** uses data, statistical, and machine learning techniques to extract insights and knowledge from structured and unstructured data sets. This includes collecting, cleaning, and analyzing large amounts of data, developing predictive models, and communicating findings to stakeholders. To be successful as a Data Scientist, an individual should have a strong understanding of statistics, machine learning, and programming concepts. Additionally, they should have experience with various data analysis tools and programming languages such as Python, R, and SQL. Good problem-solving and communication skills are also crucial as Data Scientists often need to explain complex technical concepts to non-technical stakeholders. Data science is a rapidly growing field, and there is a high demand for professionals who can extract insights from data. A career as a Data Scientist can be a challenging and rewarding opportunity for individuals interested in using data to drive decision-making and are passionate about turning data into actionable insights.

Data scientists use their mathematics, statistics, and computer science expertise to extract insights and knowledge from large and complex data sets. They are critical in helping organizations make data-driven decisions and gain a competitive advantage.

Degrees and certifications required: Many Data Scientists have a bachelor's or master's degree in computer science, information technology, mathematics, statistics, or a related field. In addition, certifications such as Certified Analytics Professional (CAP) and Azure Data Scientist Associate can benefit individuals seeking to demonstrate their data science expertise.

Job growth projections: The demand for Data Scientists are expected to grow in the coming years as organizations increasingly recognize the importance of data-driven decision-making. According to the Bureau of Labor Statistics (BLS), the employment of computer and information research scientists, which includes Data Scientists, is projected to grow 16 percent from 2019 to 2029, faster than the average for all occupations.

Advancement opportunities: Data Scientists can advance their careers by taking on more organizational responsibilities, such as leading data analytics projects or mentoring junior data scientists. With experience and expertise, they can move into management roles, such as data analytics manager or chief data officer. They may also move into related fields, such as machine learning or artificial intelligence, where they can specialize in specific data analysis and technology areas.

4.12. **DevOps Engineer** is a rapidly growing field, becoming increasingly important for organizations looking to deliver software faster while maintaining high availability and reliability. DevOps Engineer is responsible for designing, implementing, and maintaining the infrastructure and tools that support the software development process. This includes tasks such as automating the deployment and scaling of applications, monitoring, and troubleshooting systems and collaborating with development teams to improve the overall efficiency and reliability of the software development process. To succeed as a DevOps Engineer, an individual should have a strong understanding of systems administration and automation and experience with various technologies such as Linux, AWS, and Docker. Additionally, DevOps Engineers should have strong problem-solving and communication skills, the ability to work well in a team environment, and knowledge of software development methodologies, such as Agile and Scrum. A career as a DevOps Engineer can be a challenging and rewarding opportunity for individuals interested in technology and passionate about collaboration and continuous improvement.

Degrees and certifications required: While there is no specific degree or certification needed to work in DevOps, many professionals in this field have a background in computer science, software engineering, or a related field. Certifications such as Certified DevOps Professional (CDP) and AWS Certified DevOps Engineer can demonstrate a professional's expertise in DevOps and help with advancement opportunities.

Job growth projections: The demand for DevOps professionals is growing as organizations adopt a DevOps approach to software development. According to the BLS, employment of computer and information research scientists, which includes some DevOps roles, is projected to grow 16 percent from 2019 to 2029, faster than the average for all occupations.

Advancement opportunities: DevOps practitioners can advance their careers by taking on more organizational responsibilities, such as leading DevOps teams or working on larger, more complex projects. With experience, they can move into management roles, such as DevOps manager or IT director, where they can oversee the DevOps process and implement strategies for continuous improvement. They may also choose to specialize in a specific area of DevOps, such as security or cloud computing, and move into related fields.

4.13. **DevSecOps Engineer** is a relatively new role that combines elements of software development, security, and operations, focusing on integrating security into the software development process from the earliest stages and automating security testing and remediation. It aims to provide security and development teams with the tools and techniques to work together effectively to build and deploy secure software quickly and efficiently. Being a DevSecOps Engineer can be a challenging and rewarding career for detail-oriented individuals. They play a critical role in the development and success of technology companies. They ensure that security is integrated into the software development process and that vulnerabilities are identified and addressed quickly. To be successful as a DevSecOps Engineer, an individual should have a strong understanding of software development, security, and operations.

Additionally, they should have strong analytical, problem-solving, and communication skills. They should be able to work well with cross-functional teams and handle complex projects and people. Familiarity with different security tools and technologies is a must.

Degrees and certifications required: A bachelor's degree in computer science, software engineering, or a related field is the standard for DevSecOps Engineers. Professional certifications in information security, such as Certified Information Systems Security Professional (CISSP), Certified Ethical Hacker (CEH), and CompTIA Security+, can demonstrate a professional's expertise in security and help with advancement opportunities.

Job growth projections: The demand for professionals with expertise in DevSecOps is growing as organizations seek to improve their security posture and respond to increasing security threats. The global DevSecOps market is anticipated to register a CAGR of 32.2 percent over the next few years. Revenue is projected to grow from USD 2.55 billion in 2020 to USD 23.42 billion in 2028.

Advancement opportunities: DevSecOps Engineers can advance their careers by taking on more organizational responsibilities, such as leading DevSecOps teams or working on larger, more complex projects. With experience, they may move into management roles, such as DevSecOps Manager or Information Security Officer, where they can oversee the DevSecOps process and implement strategies for continuous improvement. They may also specialize in a specific security area, such as cloud or application security, and move into related fields.

Chapter FIVE

Careers in Financial Technology (FinTech)

Objectives

1. Introduction to FinTech
2. List of trending careers
3. Degrees and certifications required
4. Job growth projections
5. Advancement opportunities

Financial Technology (FinTech) is a rapidly growing field encompassing many careers that involve applying technology to financial services. FinTech companies, often start-ups, use innovative technology to disrupt traditional financial systems and services in banking, payments, insurance, and investment. These companies leverage technology to provide financial services more efficiently, at a lower cost, and to a broader population than traditional financial institutions. FinTech careers offer diverse options and skill sets, from software development and data analytics to risk management and compliance. These careers include FinTech consultant, FinTech software

44

developer, FinTech data scientist, and FinTech product manager. Some jobs may require a background in finance and a degree in finance or business, while others may require a technical experience in computer science or engineering. FinTech is a field that is at the intersection of finance and technology. Therefore many of the jobs in this field are highly interdisciplinary and require a combination of both technical and business skills. FinTech professionals can enjoy exciting career opportunities, as they can work in traditional financial institutions, FinTech start-ups, venture capital firms, or consulting firms. The following are the trending careers in the FinTech industry:

5.1. **FinTech consultant:** A FinTech consultant is an expert in the financial technology industry who advises and guides organizations looking to improve their financial systems and processes. FinTech consultants are in high demand as the financial services industry continues to evolve rapidly and adopt new technologies.

Degrees and certifications required: Many FinTech consultants hold a bachelor's or master's degree in finance, economics, computer science, or a related field. In addition, some may choose to obtain professional certifications in finance, such as the Chartered Financial

Analyst (CFA) or Financial Risk Manager (FRM), or in technology, such as Certified Information Systems Auditor (CISA), Professional Scrum Master or Certified Scrum Master (CSM).

Job growth projections: The global FinTech market is expected to grow rapidly in the coming years, driven by the increasing adoption of digital financial services and new technologies such as artificial intelligence and blockchain. This growth is expected to create significant demand for FinTech consultants who can help organizations navigate the rapidly evolving financial technology landscape.

Advancement opportunities: FinTech consultants can advance their careers by taking on more responsibility and working on larger, more complex projects. With experience, they may move into senior consulting roles, such as Senior FinTech Consultant or FinTech Practice Lead, where they can lead teams and provide high-level strategic guidance. Some may also choose to specialize in a specific area of finance or technology, such as digital payments or blockchain, and move into related fields.

5.2. **FinTech Software Developer:** A FinTech software developer is a software engineer who specializes

in developing financial technology (FinTech) applications and systems. They play a critical role in driving innovation and improving the efficiency of financial services.

Degrees and certifications required: To become a FinTech software developer, a bachelor's or master's degree in computer science, software engineering, or a related field is typically required. Some FinTech software developers may choose to obtain certifications in specific technologies, such as Certified Java Developer (CJD) or Certified Blockchain Developer (CBD). In addition, it's also beneficial to have experience with programming languages and technologies commonly used in the FinTech industry, such as Java, Python, and blockchain.

Job growth projections: The FinTech industry's growth will drive demand for skilled software developers in the coming years. The increasing use of technology in finance, such as digital payments, online banking, and robo-advisors, is creating new opportunities for FinTech software developers to design and develop innovative solutions.

Advancement opportunities: FinTech software developers can advance their careers by taking on more complex projects and responsibilities, such as leading development teams or working on strategic initiatives. With experience and expertise, they can also transition into senior software development roles, such as Lead FinTech Software Developer or FinTech Technical Architect. Some may also choose to specialize in a specific area of FinTech, such as mobile banking or cryptocurrency, and move into related fields.

5.3. **FinTech Data Scientist**: A FinTech data scientist is a data professional who analyzes and interprets data in the financial technology (FinTech) industry. They use their data analysis and machine learning expertise to help organizations make informed decisions and drive innovation in the financial services sector.

Degrees and certifications required: To become a FinTech data scientist, a bachelor's or master's degree in computer science, data science, mathematics, statistics, or a related field is typically required. In addition, experience with data analysis and machine learning techniques, as well as proficiency in programming languages such as Python, R, and SQL, is essential. Some FinTech data scientists may also choose to obtain certifications in specific technologies or methodologies, such as Certified Analytics Professional (CAP) or Certified Big Data Professional (CBDP).

Job growth projections: The demand for FinTech data scientists is expected to grow in the coming years as organizations increasingly seek to leverage data and analytics to drive innovation and improve their operations. The increasing use of technology in finance, such as digital payments, online banking, and robo-advisors, is creating new opportunities for FinTech data scientists to use their skills to drive innovation in the financial services sector.

Advancement opportunities: FinTech data scientists can advance their careers by taking on more complex projects and responsibilities, such as leading data science teams or working on strategic initiatives. With experience and expertise, they can also transition into senior data science roles, such as FinTech Data Science Manager or FinTech Chief Data Scientist. Some may also choose to specialize in a specific area of FinTech, such as risk management or customer analytics, and move into related fields.

5.4. **FinTech Product Manager:** A FinTech product manager is responsible for leading the development and implementation of innovative financial technology products and services. They work closely with cross-functional teams, including developers, designers, and

sales, to create and bring new products to market that meet customers' needs and drive growth for their organization.

Degrees and certifications required: A bachelor's or master's degree in business, finance, computer science, or a related field is typically needed for a career as a FinTech product manager. Additionally, experience in the FinTech industry and a strong understanding of the latest trends and technologies are essential. Some product managers may also pursue certification in product management, such as the Certified Product Manager (CPM) or Product Development Professional (PDP) certification.

Job growth projections: The demand for FinTech product managers is expected to grow as the financial technology industry continues to expand and evolve. Organizations seek experienced and knowledgeable product managers to help them bring new and innovative products to market and compete in an increasingly digital financial services landscape.

Advancement opportunities: FinTech product managers can advance their careers by taking on more complex projects and responsibilities, such as leading cross-functional teams or overseeing the development of multiple products. With experience and expertise, they can also transition into senior product management roles, such as FinTech Product Director or Chief Product Officer. Some may also choose to move into related fields, such as strategy or business development, where they can use their expertise to drive growth and innovation for their organization.

5.5. **FinTech Business Analyst:** FinTech Business Analysts are professionals who work at the intersection of finance and technology. They play a critical role in helping organizations navigate the rapidly evolving world of financial technology. These professionals evaluate FinTech products, services, and technologies and determine how they can be leveraged to drive business growth and improve financial performance. They also work closely with cross-functional teams to develop and implement FinTech solutions that meet the unique needs of their organizations. With a deep understanding of finance and technology, FinTech Business Analysts are well-positioned to play a key role in shaping the future of finance and driving innovation in the financial services industry.

Degrees and certifications required: A bachelor's degree in finance, economics, business administration, or a related field is typically needed for a career as a FinTech business analyst. Familiarity with FinTech products, technologies, and trends is also essential. In addition, certifications in business analysis, such as the Certified Business Analysis Professional (CBAP), can be advantageous.

Job growth projections: The FinTech industry is rapidly growing and is expected to grow in the coming years. This means there will likely be an increased demand for FinTech business analysts who can help organizations navigate the complex and rapidly evolving world of financial technology.

Advancement opportunities: A career as a FinTech business analyst can lead to various advancement opportunities. With experience and demonstrated expertise, a FinTech business analyst can move into management positions, such as a product manager or project manager, or take on more complex and strategic roles, such as a consultant or advisor. Additionally, there is a growing need for FinTech and digital transformation experts, which can provide further opportunities for advancement.

5.6. **FinTech Compliance Officer**: A FinTech Compliance Officer is a professional who works in the financial technology sector and ensures that a company's operations comply with applicable laws and regulations. In this role, individuals must understand financial regulations, be highly organized, and possess excellent communication and interpersonal skills. They play a critical role in ensuring that the company operates ethically and responsibly and that its financial products and services meet industry standards. With the increasing complexity of financial regulations and the growing importance of compliance in the financial sector, a career as a FinTech Compliance Officer can be challenging and rewarding.

Degrees and certifications required: A bachelor's degree in a relevant field such as finance, law, or business is often a minimum requirement for a FinTech Compliance Officer. However, many employers prefer candidates with a master's degree in a relevant field. Additionally, certifications such as the Certified Regulatory Compliance Manager (CRCM) or Certified Financial Services Auditor (CFSA) can be beneficial.

Job growth projections: The demand for FinTech Compliance Officers is growing rapidly, driven by the increasing popularity of financial technology and the growing need for organizations to comply with regulations and protect their customer's financial data. According to the Bureau of Labor Statistics, employment in compliance and regulatory affairs is projected to grow 7 percent from

2019 to 2029, faster than the average for all occupations. With the increasing importance of compliance and regulatory affairs in the FinTech industry, there are ample opportunities for growth and advancement for talented and motivated FinTech Compliance Officers.

Advancement opportunities: FinTech Compliance Officers typically start their careers as compliance analysts or officers and can progress to more senior roles such as chief compliance officers or regulatory affairs directors. Some may also choose to specialize in a specific area of compliance, such as anti-money laundering or cyber security, and pursue related certifications and advanced degrees.

5.7. **FinTech Risk Manager**: A FinTech Risk Manager plays a critical role in the financial technology industry by assessing and mitigating various financial products and services risks. They ensure that a company's operations are conducted safely and securely and that its customers' assets and information are protected. With the rapid growth of the financial technology sector and the increasing number of innovative financial products and services, a career as a FinTech Risk Manager is both challenging and rewarding.

Degrees and Certifications: A bachelor's degree in finance, economics, or a related field is typically required to become a FinTech Risk Manager. Additionally, certifications such as the Financial Risk Manager (FRM) designation, the Professional Risk Manager (PRM) designation, or the Certified Financial Analyst (CFA) designation may be preferred or required. Some employers may also prefer or require a master's degree in a related field.

Job Growth Projections: The demand for FinTech Risk Managers is expected to grow in the coming years as the financial technology sector continues to expand and evolve. According to the Bureau of Labor Statistics, employment of financial managers is projected to grow 7 percent from 2019 to 2029, which is about as fast as the average for all occupations.

Advancement Opportunities: As FinTech Risk Manager gains experience and knowledge, they may have the opportunity to advance to senior-level positions within their organization, such as a Chief Risk Officer or a Risk Management Director. Additionally, they may be able to work for a larger financial technology firm or a consulting firm specializing in risk management services. With continued education and professional development,

FinTech Risk Managers can position themselves for long-term career growth and advancement in the financial technology sector.

5.8.   **FinTech Sales and Marketing:** FinTech Sales and Marketing is a rapidly growing field that combines finance and technology to create innovative financial products and services. As FinTech Sales and Marketing professionals, they are responsible for promoting and selling cutting-edge financial technologies to businesses and consumers. In this role, they are essential in helping shape the financial industry's future.

Degrees and certifications required: A bachelor's degree in finance, marketing, business administration, or a related field is typically required for entry-level positions in FinTech Sales and Marketing. In addition, certifications in digital marketing, such as the Google Analytics Individual Qualification, can be beneficial.

Job growth projections: The FinTech industry is rapidly expanding, and the demand for skilled sales and marketing professionals is increasing. According to recent data, the global FinTech market is expected to grow significantly in the coming years, providing ample opportunities for growth and advancement.

Advancement opportunities: There is a high demand for skilled professionals in the FinTech Sales and Marketing industry, and many opportunities for career advancement. With experience and the right skills, you can progress to more senior roles such as FinTech Sales Manager, FinTech Marketing Director, or FinTech Business Development Manager. Additionally, there is always the possibility of starting your own FinTech Company.

5.9. FinTech Project Manager:
A FinTech Project Manager oversees specific short-term financial technology projects' planning, implementation, and tracking. They work with cross-functional teams to deliver projects that support business goals and objectives, including business stakeholders, software developers, and quality assurance specialists.

Degrees and certifications required: A finance, business, or computer science bachelor's degree is often needed for a FinTech Project Manager role. Some employers may prefer a master's degree in business administration (MBA) or a related field. Additionally, certifications such as Project Management Professional (PMP), Professional Scrum Master, or Certified Scrum

Master (CSM) can be valuable for those looking to enhance their skills and knowledge in project management.

Job growth projections: The demand for FinTech Project Managers is growing as financial technology plays a larger role in the financial services industry. According to the Bureau of Labor Statistics, employment in the financial services sector is expected to grow 7 percent from 2019 to 2029, faster than the average for all occupations.

Advancement opportunities: A successful FinTech Project Manager can advance to senior project management roles or pursue higher-level management positions, such as program manager or portfolio manager. They may also explore opportunities in related fields such as consulting or business analysis. With the growing demand for financial technology, there will likely be a wealth of advancement opportunities for FinTech Project Managers in the future.

5.10. **FinTech Network Engineer:** A FinTech Network Engineer is a highly skilled professional responsible for designing, implementing, and maintaining the network infrastructure of a financial technology company. They play a critical role in ensuring the security, reliability, and performance of the network, which is essential for the smooth functioning of the financial

services offered by the organization. The role of a FinTech Network Engineer is to stay ahead of the curve in terms of technology and regulatory requirements and ensure that the network can support the company's business goals.

Degrees and Certifications: A bachelor's degree in Computer Science, Information Technology, or a related field is typically required for this role. In addition, certifications such as Cisco Certified Network Associate (CCNA) or Certified Ethical Hacker (CEH) can be valuable for a FinTech Network Engineer. Hands-on experience working with network infrastructure, security, and cloud technologies is also highly desirable.

Job Growth Projections: The demand for FinTech Network Engineers is expected to grow in the coming years as the financial services industry continues to adopt technology and expand its digital offerings. This, in turn, is expected to create new job opportunities for individuals with network engineering and security expertise.

Advancement Opportunities: There are several career paths available for FinTech Network Engineers, including opportunities for advancement into more senior roles such as Network Security Engineer, Cloud Network Engineer, or Network and Information Security Manager. As technology continues to evolve and the demand for highly skilled network professionals increases, there is significant potential for career growth and advancement for individuals in this field.

Chapter SIX

IT Industry Careers for Non-Technical Professionals

Objectives

1. Introduction to Non-Technical IT
2. List of Trending Careers
3. Degrees and certifications required
4. Job growth projections
5. Advancement opportunities

The Information Technology (IT) industry includes a variety of non-technical roles that play a crucial role in the success of technology companies and organizations. For example, according to the Project Management Institute (PMI), the demand for project managers with experience in the technology industry is expected to grow in the coming years. (PMI, 2020). Similarly, research from the International Institute of Business Analysis (IIBA) suggests that the business analyst role is becoming increasingly important in the technology industry as organizations look to improve their processes and drive innovation. (IIBA, 2019).

Non-technical IT careers can be an excellent fit for individuals with various skills, backgrounds, and interests. These roles often require strong analytical, problem-solving, and communication skills and the ability to work well in a team. Additionally, many non-technical roles in the IT industry offer a high degree of flexibility, with opportunities for remote work and flexible hours. As technology continues to play an increasingly important role in the global economy, the opportunities for non-technical IT careers will likely continue to grow. These careers offer a chance to work in an exciting, dynamic, and rapidly evolving industry while providing the potential for a well-paying and satisfying job. The following are the trending non-technical IT careers:

6.1. **Scrum Master** is a non-technical IT industry role related explicitly to Agile software development methodologies. The Scrum Master is responsible for facilitating and leading the Scrum team, which includes developers, product owners, and other stakeholders. Their primary focus is ensuring that the team adheres to the Scrum framework and everyone follows the Agile principles and values. Some of the responsibilities of a Scrum Master include:

✓ Facilitating Scrum ceremonies, such as sprint planning, daily stand-ups, sprint retrospectives, and sprint reviews,

✓ Removing obstacles that might be impeding the team's progress,

✓ Helping to create and maintain a positive and productive team culture,

✓ Coaching team members on Scrum practices and principles,

✓ Working with the product owner to prioritize the backlog and ensure the team works on the most critical tasks.

Being a Scrum Master can be a rewarding career for individuals passionate about Agile software development who want to help teams work together effectively and efficiently, improve their productivity, and continuously deliver value. Scrum Masters work closely with teams and help facilitate communication, collaboration, and teamwork, which leads to successful projects. To be successful as a Scrum Master, an individual should have a strong understanding of Agile methodologies and Scrum framework, as well as experience with software development and software project management. Additionally, they should have strong communication, problem-solving, and leadership skills. Scrum Masters should also be highly adaptable, as they must be able to work in various roles and handle obstacles and conflicts.

Degrees and Certifications Required: A Scrum Master guides and facilitates Agile development teams implementing the Scrum framework. Several certifications are available for individuals seeking to become a Scrum Master. The most recognized certifications are the Professional Scrum Master (PSM) Scrum.org and Scrum Alliance offer Certified Scrum Masters (CSM). Individuals are required to complete a two-day training course and pass an online certification exam. Some organizations may require a Bachelor's or Master's degree in a related field, such as computer science, software engineering, project management, or business administration. However, it is not a requirement, and many Scrum Masters have gained the required knowledge and skills through experience and self-study.

Job Growth Projections: The demand for Scrum Masters is growing as more organizations adopt Agile methodologies. According to the Project Management Institute, the need for Agile project management professionals is expected to grow by as much as 28 percent in the next 5-10 years. As a result, job opportunities for Scrum Masters are expected to increase as organizations seek to adopt Agile practices and principles to improve their project delivery and product development.

Advancement Opportunities: A Scrum Master can advance their career in several ways. They can become an Agile coach, helping organizations to adopt Agile methodologies, practices, and principles. They can also move into management positions within an Agile development team or an IT organization. Additionally, Scrum Masters can pursue certifications such as the Certified Scrum Professional (CSP) or the Certified Enterprise Coach (CEC) to demonstrate their expertise and advance their careers.

6.2. **Product Manager** is a non-technical role in the IT industry responsible for developing and succeeding in a company's product offering. The Product Manager is responsible for defining the product vision, strategy, and road map and ensuring that the product meets customer needs and achieves business objectives. They work with cross-functional teams, including engineering, design, marketing, sales, and customer support, to ensure the product is successfully developed, launched, and supported. Some of the responsibilities of a Product Manager include the following:

✓ Conducting market research and analyzing customer needs to inform product vision and strategy,

✓ Creating and maintaining a product roadmap,

✓ Prioritizing and managing the product backlog,

✓ Communicating the product vision and strategy to stakeholders within the company,

✓ Collaborating with sales and marketing teams to develop and execute go-to-market strategies,

✓ Tracking and analyzing product performance to ensure the product meets customer needs and business objectives.

Being a Product Manager can be a challenging and rewarding career for individuals who are passionate about technology and enjoy working with cross-functional teams to bring new products to market. Product Managers play a critical role in the development and success of technology companies, as they are responsible for defining the product strategy and ensuring that it meets customers' needs and achieves business objectives. To be successful as a Product Manager, an individual should have a strong understanding of the technology industry and the product development process, as well as experience with product management, marketing, and project management. Additionally, they should have strong analytical, problem-solving, and communication skills. A Product Manager should also have a good understanding of the market and customer needs; they must be able to use this understanding to prioritize the product backlog and guide the development of the product.

Degrees and Certifications Required: A Product Manager is responsible for the development and success of a product. A bachelor's degree is usually the minimum requirement for a Product Manager position. However, many employers prefer a Master's degree in a relevant field such as business administration, marketing, or computer science. Some employers may also require a technical background or experience in a related field.

There are several certifications available for Product Managers that can demonstrate their knowledge and skills, such as the Certified Product Manager (CPM) offered by the Association of International Product Management and Marketing (AIPMM) or the Product Manager Certificate (PMC) provided by the Product Development and Management Association (PDMA). These certifications are not required but can demonstrate a candidate's expertise and commitment to the field.

Job Growth Projections: The demand for Product Managers is growing as companies seek to develop and market products that meet the needs of their customers. According to the Bureau of Labor Statistics, the employment of Market Research Analysts and Marketing Specialists, which includes Product Managers, is projected to grow by 23 percent from 2019 to 2029, much faster than the average for all occupations. This growth is due to the increasing importance of digital marketing and the need for companies to understand their customers and markets.

Advancement Opportunities: A Product Manager can advance their career in several ways. They can move into senior-level positions such as Director of Product Management or Chief Product Officer. They can also transition into marketing, sales, or entrepreneurship. Some Product Managers may also start their own companies or work as consultants. Additionally, Product Managers can pursue advanced degrees or certifications to demonstrate their expertise and continue to grow their careers.

6.3. **Project Manager** is a non-technical role in the IT industry responsible for planning, executing, and closing IT projects on time, within budget, and to stakeholders' satisfaction. They work with cross-functional teams to ensure that the project meets its goals and objectives and that all necessary resources are acquired and allocated effectively. Some of the responsibilities of a Project Manager include the following:

✓ Defining project scope and objectives,

✓ Creating a detailed project plan and schedule,

✓ Identifying and managing project risks,

✓ Managing project resources, including a budget, team members, and equipment,

✓ Communicating project status and progress to stakeholders,

✓ Ensuring that the project meets quality standards and client requirements,

✓ Managing project changes and ensuring that they are tracked and communicated to stakeholders.

Being a Project Manager can be a challenging and rewarding career for individuals who are organized, good communicators, and enjoy leading cross-functional teams to success. Project Managers play a critical role in the development and success of technology companies, as they are responsible for ensuring the successful completion of projects and delivering value to customers, stakeholders, and the organization. To succeed as a Project Manager, an individual should have a strong understanding of project management methodologies and tools and experience managing IT projects. Additionally, they should have strong leadership, problem-solving, and communication skills. They should be able to plan effectively, allocate resources, and handle complex projects and people.

Degrees and Certifications Required: A Project Manager is responsible for planning, executing, and closing projects. A bachelor's degree is usually the minimum requirement for a Project Manager position. However, many employers prefer a Master's degree in a relevant field such as business administration, engineering, or computer science. Some employers may also require a technical background or experience in a related field.

There are several certifications available for Project Managers that can demonstrate their knowledge and skills, such as the Project Management Professional (PMP) certification offered by the Project Management Institute (PMI), the Certified Associate in Project Management (CAPM) certification provided by PMI, or the PRINCE2 (PRojects IN Controlled Environments) certification offered by Axelos. These certifications are not required but can demonstrate a candidate's expertise and commitment to the field.

Job Growth Projections: The demand for Project Managers is growing as companies seek to improve their project delivery and achieve better business results. According to the U.S. Bureau of Labor Statistics, employment of project management specialists is projected to grow 7 percent from 2021 to 2031, about as fast as the average for all occupations. However, according to the Project Management Institute (PMI), there will be a 33% increase in project management-oriented jobs in 11 countries (Australia, Brazil, Canada, China, Germany, India, Japan, Saudi Arabia, the United Arab Emirates, the United Kingdom and the United States) by 2027. This growth is due to the increasing importance of managing projects efficiently and effectively to meet the needs of businesses and organizations.

Advancement Opportunities: A Project Manager can move into senior-level positions such as Director of Project Management, Program Manager, or Portfolio Manager. They can also transition into other related fields, such as consulting, business operations, or program management. Additionally, Project Managers can pursue advanced degrees or certifications to demonstrate their expertise and continue to grow their careers.

6.4. **Business Analyst (BA)** is a non-technical role in the IT industry. It is responsible for identifying and analyzing business needs and problems, then designing and implementing solutions to address them. They work closely with cross-functional teams, including IT, finance, and operations, to understand business processes and systems and identify improvement opportunities. Some of the responsibilities of a Business Analyst include the following:

✓ Gathering and analyzing business requirements from stakeholders,

✓ Identifying business problems and opportunities for improvement,

✓ Designing solutions to address business needs, including process and system changes,

✓ Developing functional and technical specifications,

✓ Communicating business requirements to IT and other teams,

✓ Testing and validating solutions to ensure they meet business needs,

✓ Supporting the implementation and rollout of new solutions.

Being a Business Analyst can be a challenging and rewarding career for detail-oriented individuals and good communicators who enjoy solving complex problems. Business Analysts play a critical role in the development and success of technology companies. They are responsible for understanding and analyzing the business needs and defining solutions that deliver value to the organization and its customers. To succeed as a Business Analyst, an individual should have a strong understanding of business processes and systems and experience gathering and analyzing requirements and designing and implementing solutions. Additionally, they should have strong analytical, problem-solving, and communication skills. They should be able to work well with cross-functional teams and handle complex projects and people.

Degrees and Certifications Required: A Business Analyst (BA) is responsible for helping organizations improve their processes and systems to meet the needs of their stakeholders. A bachelor's degree is usually the minimum requirement for a Business Analyst position. However, many employers prefer a Master's degree in a relevant field such as business administration, computer science, or engineering. Some employers may also require a technical background or experience in a related field.

Degrees and Certifications Required: There are several certifications available for Business Analysts that can demonstrate their knowledge and skills, such as the Certified Business Analysis Professional (CBAP) certification offered by the International Institute of Business Analysis (IIBA), the Professional in Business Analysis (PBA) certification provided by IIBA, or the Certified Analytics Professional (CAP) certification offered by the Institute for Operations Research and the Management Sciences (INFORMS). These certifications are not required but can demonstrate a candidate's expertise and commitment to the field.

Job Growth Projections: The demand for Business Analysts is growing as organizations seek to improve their processes and systems to meet the needs of their stakeholders. According to the Bureau of Labor Statistics, employment of Management Analysts, which includes Business Analysts, is projected to grow 14 percent from 2019 to 2029, much faster than the average for all occupations. This growth is due to the increasing importance of data and analytics in decision-making and the need for organizations to improve their processes and systems.

Advancement Opportunities: Business Analysts can advance their careers in several ways. They can move into senior-level positions such as Manager of Business

Analysis, Director of Business Transformation, or Chief Analytics Officer. They can also transition into other related fields, such as management consulting, data science, or project management. Additionally, Business Analysts can pursue advanced degrees or certifications to demonstrate their expertise and continue to grow their careers.

6.5. **IT Sales and Marketing** is a non-technical role in the IT industry responsible for promoting and selling products or services to customers. They work with cross-functional teams, including product development, engineering, and customer support, to understand the company's product offering and to develop effective sales and marketing strategies. Some of the responsibilities of an IT Sales and Marketing professional include the following:

✓ Identifying and targeting potential customers,

✓ Building and maintaining relationships with customers,

✓ Creating and delivering presentations and demonstrations of the company's products or services,

✓ Negotiating and closing sales deals,

✓ Developing and implementing marketing campaigns,

✓ Analyzing sales and marketing data to measure the effectiveness of campaigns and adjust strategies as needed.

Being an IT Sales and Marketing professional can be a challenging and rewarding career for highly motivated individuals, good communicators, and enjoy building relationships with customers. They play a critical role in the development and success of technology companies as they promote and sell products or services, identify potential customers, and build long-term relationships. To be successful as an IT Sales and Marketing professional, an individual should have a strong understanding of the technology industry and experience in sales and marketing. Additionally, they should have strong communication, negotiation, and interpersonal skills. They should be able to work well with cross-functional teams and handle complex projects and people.

Degrees and Certifications Required: IT Sales and Marketing professionals promote and sell technology products and services to customers. A bachelor's degree is usually the minimum requirement for an IT Sales and Marketing position. However, many employers prefer a degree in a relevant field such as business administration, marketing, or computer science. Some employers may also require experience in technology sales or marketing.

There are several certifications available for IT Sales and Marketing professionals that can demonstrate their knowledge and skills, such as the Certified Information Systems Security Professional (CISSP) certification offered by (ISC)², the Certified Marketing Professional (CMP) certification provided by the Association of National Advertisers (ANA), or the Power Platform Fundamentals certification provided by Microsoft. These certifications are not required but can demonstrate a candidate's expertise and commitment to the field.

Job Growth Projections: The demand for IT Sales and Marketing professionals is growing as companies seek to increase their market share and revenue in the technology industry. The Bureau of Labor Statistics projects that jobs for marketing and advertising managers will grow by 10 percent from 2021 to 2031, which is faster than the average growth rate for all occupations, This growth is due to the increasing importance of technology in businesses and organizations and the need for companies to promote and sell their products and services effectively.

Advancement Opportunities: IT Sales and marketing professionals can advance their careers in several ways. They can move into senior-level positions such as Director of Sales and Marketing, Vice President of Sales, or Chief Marketing Officer. They can also transition into related fields like product management, market research, or business development. Additionally, IT Sales and Marketing professionals can pursue advanced degrees or certifications to demonstrate their expertise and continue to grow their careers.

6.6. **IT Service Management (ITSM) Analyst**

is a non-technical role in the IT industry responsible for managing and improving the delivery of IT services to customers. They work with cross-functional teams, including IT operations, development, and support, to ensure that IT services meet the needs of customers and the organization. Some of the responsibilities of an ITSM Analyst include the following:

✓ Supporting the implementation and maintenance of IT service management frameworks, such as the IT Infrastructure Library (ITIL),

✓ Managing and monitoring IT service performance to ensure that service-level agreements (SLAs) and service-level objectives (SLOs) are met,

- ✓ Identifying and analyzing service-related issues and working with teams to resolve them,
- ✓ Developing and implementing service improvement plans,
- ✓ Tracking and reporting on service-related metrics,
- ✓ Developing and maintaining service-related documentation,
- ✓ Communicating service-related information to stakeholders.

Being an ITSM Analyst can be a challenging and rewarding career for detail-oriented individuals and good communicators who enjoy working with cross-functional teams to improve service delivery. They play a critical role in the development and success of technology companies. They are responsible for ensuring that IT services meet the needs of customers and the organization and for identifying and resolving service-related issues. To succeed as an ITSM Analyst, an individual should understand IT service management frameworks and methodologies, such as ITIL, and experience managing and monitoring IT services. Additionally, they should have strong analytical, problem-solving, and communication skills. They should be able to work well with cross-functional teams and handle complex projects and people.

Degrees and Certifications Required: IT Service Management (ITSM) Analysts are responsible for managing and delivering IT services to customers within an organization. A bachelor's degree in computer science, information technology, or a related field is usually required for an ITSM Analyst position. Some employers may also prefer candidates with a master's degree in a relevant field.

Several certifications are available for ITSM Analysts, such as the ITIL Foundation certification offered by Axelos, the Certified Information Systems Auditor (CISA) certification offered by ISACA, or the Certified in the Governance of Enterprise IT (CGEIT) certification offered by ISACA. These certifications demonstrate a candidate's expertise in IT service management and commitment to the field.

Job Growth Projections: The demand for ITSM Analysts is growing as organizations seek to improve their IT service delivery and management. According to the Bureau of Labor Statistics, employment of computer and information systems managers, which includes ITSM Analysts, is projected to grow 11 percent from 2019 to 2029, much faster than the average for all occupations. This growth is due to the increasing importance of technology in businesses and organizations and the need for effective IT service delivery and management.

Advancement Opportunities: An ITSM Analyst can move into senior-level positions such as IT Service Management Manager or Director of IT Service Management. They can also transition into related fields such as IT security, project management, or business analysis. Additionally, ITSM Analysts can pursue advanced degrees or certifications to demonstrate their expertise and continue to grow their careers.

6.7. **IT Procurement** is a non-technical role in the IT industry responsible for purchasing an organization's goods and services. They work closely with cross-functional teams, including IT, finance, and operations, to identify and evaluate suppliers, negotiate contracts, and ensure that the organization gets the best value for its purchases. Some of the responsibilities of an IT Procurement professional include the following:

✓ Identifying and evaluating potential suppliers,
✓ Negotiating contracts and pricing for goods and services,
✓ Managing and maintaining supplier relationships,

- ✓ Ensuring compliance with procurement policies and procedures,
- ✓ Managing the purchasing process from requisition to invoice payment,
- ✓ Monitoring and analyzing supplier performance,
- ✓ Communicating with internal stakeholders to understand their needs and requirements.

Being an IT Procurement professional can be a challenging and rewarding career for detail-oriented individuals and good communicators who enjoy working with cross-functional teams. They play a critical role in the development and success of technology companies, ensuring that the organization is getting the best value for its purchases, managing relationships with suppliers, and interpreting internal stakeholders' needs. To be successful as an IT Procurement professional, an individual should have a strong understanding of the technology industry and experience in procurement, purchasing, and supplier management. Additionally, they should have strong analytical, negotiation, and interpersonal skills. They should be able to work well with cross-functional teams and handle complex projects and people.

Degrees and Certifications Required: IT Procurement refers to acquiring technology-related products and services for an organization. A bachelor's degree in business administration, supply chain management, or a related field is usually required for an IT Procurement role. Some employers may also prefer candidates with a master's degree in a relevant field.

There are several certifications available for IT Procurement professionals, such as the Certified Purchasing Manager (CPM) certification offered by the Institute for Supply Management (ISM), the Certified Professional in Supply Management (CPSM) certification provided by ISM, or the Chartered Institute of Procurement & Supply (CIPS) qualifications. These certifications demonstrate a candidate's procurement and supply chain management expertise and commitment to the field.

Job Growth Projections: The demand for IT Procurement professionals is growing as organizations seek to improve their technology-related procurement processes. According to the Bureau of Labor Statistics, employment of purchasing managers, buyers, and purchasing agents, including IT Procurement professionals, is projected to grow 6 percent from 2019 to 2031, faster than the average for all occupations. This growth is due to the increasing importance of technology in businesses and organizations and the need for effective procurement processes.

Advancement Opportunities: An IT Procurement professional can advance their career in several ways. They can move into senior-level positions such as IT Procurement Manager or Director of IT Procurement. They can also transition into related fields such as supply chain management, project management, or business analysis. Additionally, IT Procurement professionals can pursue advanced degrees or certifications to demonstrate their expertise and continue to grow their careers.

6.8. **IT Risk Manager** is a non-technical role in the IT industry responsible for identifying, assessing, and managing IT systems and processes risks. They work with cross-functional teams, including IT, compliance, and business units, to develop and implement strategies to mitigate and manage risks. Some of the responsibilities of an IT Risk Manager include the following:

✓ Identifying and assessing risks associated with IT systems and processes,

✓ Developing and implementing risk management plans,

✓ Monitoring and reporting on risks and risk management activities,

- ✓ Coordinating with other teams, such as IT and compliance, to ensure compliance with regulations and standards,
- ✓ Communicating with stakeholders about risks and risk management activities,
- ✓ Providing training and guidance to staff on risk management,
- ✓ Keeping up-to-date with laws, regulations, and industry standards related to IT risk management.

Being an IT Risk Manager can be a challenging and rewarding career for detail-oriented individuals and good communicators who enjoy working with cross-functional teams to identify and manage risks. They play a critical role in the development and success of technology companies, ensuring that the organization's IT systems and processes comply with laws and regulations and protect against potential risks. To succeed as an IT Risk Manager, an individual should have a strong understanding of IT risk management frameworks and methodologies and experience in assessing and managing risks. Additionally, they should have strong analytical, problem-solving, and communication skills. They must work well with cross-functional teams and handle complex projects and people.

Degrees and Certifications Required: An IT Risk Manager is responsible for identifying, evaluating, and managing the risks associated with an organization's technology systems and processes. A bachelor's degree in a relevant field, such as computer science, information technology, or business administration, is typically required. Many IT Risk Managers also hold advanced degrees, such as a master's in business administration (MBA) or a master's in information security.

There are several certifications available for IT Risk Managers, such as the Certified Information Systems Security Professional (CISSP) certification offered by (ISC)², the Certified in the Governance of Enterprise IT (CGEIT) certification offered by ISACA, or the Certified Information Security Manager (CISM) certification offered by ISACA. These certifications demonstrate a candidate's expertise in information security and commitment to the field.

Job Growth Projections: The demand for IT Risk Managers is growing as organizations seek to protect their technology systems and data from cyber-attacks, breaches, and other security risks. According to the Bureau of Labor Statistics, employment of computer and information systems managers, which includes IT Risk Managers, is projected to grow 11 percent from 2019 to 2029, much faster than the average for all occupations.

Advancement Opportunities: An IT Risk Manager can advance their career in several ways. They can move into senior-level positions such as Chief Information Security Officer (CISO) or Director of Information Security. They can also transition into related fields such as information security or project management. Additionally, IT Risk Managers can pursue advanced degrees or certifications to demonstrate their expertise and continue to grow their careers.

6.9. IT Compliance Officer is a non-technical role

in the IT industry that ensures that an organization's IT systems and processes comply with laws, regulations, and industry standards. They work closely with cross-functional teams, including IT, legal, and business units, to develop and implement compliance policies and procedures, monitor compliance, and ensure the organization meets its obligations. Some of the responsibilities of an IT Compliance Officer include the following:

✓ Identifying and assessing laws, regulations, and industry standards that apply to the organization's IT systems and processes,

- ✓ Developing and implementing policies and procedures to ensure compliance,
- ✓ Monitoring and reporting on compliance,
- ✓ Coordinating with other teams, such as IT and legal, to ensure compliance with regulations and standards,
- ✓ Communicating with stakeholders about compliance and compliance-related activities,
- ✓ Providing training and guidance to staff on compliance,
- ✓ Keeping up-to-date with laws, regulations, and industry standards related to IT compliance.

Being an IT Compliance Officer can be a challenging and rewarding career for detail-oriented individuals. They play a critical role in the development and success of technology companies. They ensure that the organization's IT systems and processes comply with laws and regulations to protect against potential risks. To succeed as an IT Compliance Officer, an individual should have a strong understanding of IT laws, regulations, and industry standards and experience developing and implementing compliance policies and procedures. Additionally, they should have strong analytical, problem-solving, and communication skills. They must work well with cross-functional teams and handle complex projects and people.

Degrees and Certifications Required: An IT Risk Manager is responsible for identifying, evaluating, and managing the risks associated with an organization's technology systems and processes. A bachelor's degree in a relevant field, such as computer science, information technology, or business administration, is typically required. Many IT Risk Managers also hold advanced degrees, such as a master's in business administration (MBA) or a master's in information security.

There are several certifications available for IT Risk Managers, such as the Certified Information Systems Security Professional (CISSP) certification offered by (ISC)², the Certified in the Governance of Enterprise IT (CGEIT) certification offered by ISACA, or the Certified Information Security Manager (CISM) certification offered by ISACA. These certifications demonstrate a candidate's expertise in information security and commitment to the field.

Job Growth Projections: The demand for IT Risk Managers is growing as organizations seek to protect their technology systems and data from cyber-attacks, breaches, and other security risks. According to the Bureau of Labor Statistics, employment of computer and information systems managers, which includes IT Risk Managers, is projected to grow 11 percent from 2019 to 2029, much faster than the average for all occupations.

Advancement Opportunities: An IT Risk Manager can advance their career in several ways. They can move into senior-level positions such as Chief Information Security Officer (CISO) or Director of Information Security. They can also transition into related fields such as information security or project management. Additionally, IT Risk Managers can pursue advanced degrees or certifications to demonstrate their expertise and continue to grow their careers.

6.10. **IT Human Resources (HR)** is a non-technical role in the IT industry that oversees and manages the human resources functions within an organization's IT department. They work closely with cross-functional teams, including IT, management, and legal, to implement and maintain policies and procedures, recruit and hire staff, and ensure that the organization complies with relevant laws and regulations. Some of the responsibilities of an IT HR professional include the following:

✓ Developing and implementing policies and procedures for the IT department,

✓ Recruiting and hiring staff for the IT department,

- ✓ Managing employee relations and addressing issues that arise,
- ✓ Ensuring compliance with relevant laws and regulations,
- ✓ Managing and maintaining employee records,
- ✓ Communicating with stakeholders about HR-related activities,
- ✓ Providing training and guidance to staff on HR-related topics.

Being an IT Human Resources (HR) professional can be a challenging and rewarding career for detail-oriented individuals. These good communicators enjoy working with cross-functional teams to manage and maintain the human resources functions within the IT department. They play a critical role in the development and success of technology companies, ensuring the organization complies with relevant laws and regulations and managing IT staff recruitment, hiring, and employment. To be successful as an IT Human Resources (HR) professional, an individual should have a strong understanding of human resources management and be familiar with relevant laws and regulations. Additionally, they should have strong analytical, problem-solving, and communication skills.

They should be able to work well with cross-functional teams and handle complex projects and people.

These are just a few examples of the many non-technical careers in the IT industry. Each role can have different responsibilities and qualifications, depending on the company and its needs. However, all of them offer a chance to work in an exciting, dynamic, and rapidly evolving industry and participate in a valuable way in the success of the organizations.

Degrees and Certifications Required: IT Human Resources (HR) professionals manage and recruit technology talent and ensure that HR policies and processes align with an organization's technology strategy. IT HR positions typically require a bachelor's degree in human resources management, business administration, or a related field. Some IT HR professionals also hold advanced degrees, such as a master's in human resources management or a master's in business administration.

Certifications in HR can be valuable for IT HR professionals, such as the Society for Human Resource Management Certified Professional (SHRM-CP) or the Human Resources Certification Institute's (HRCI) Professional in Human Resources (PHR) certification. These certifications demonstrate a candidate's knowledge and expertise in HR practices and can provide an advantage in the job market.

Job Growth Projections: The demand for IT HR professionals is growing as organizations seek to attract, retain, and manage technology talent effectively. According to the Bureau of Labor Statistics, employment of human resources specialists is projected to grow 8 percent from 2021 to 2031, faster than the average for all occupations. The HR sector has seen a 105.8 percent growth since February 2020, beating out software development as one of the most in-demand jobs in the USA.

Advancement Opportunities: IT HR professionals can move into senior-level positions such as HR Director or Chief Talent Officer. They can also transition into related fields such as talent management, organizational development, or executive recruiting. Additionally, IT HR professionals can pursue advanced degrees or certifications to demonstrate their expertise and continue to grow their careers.

Chapter SEVEN

Medical IT Career Opportunities

1. Introduction to Medical IT Career opportunities
2. Degrees and certifications required
3. Job growth projections
4. Advancement opportunities

The healthcare industry has undergone significant changes in recent years, with technology playing a major role in driving advancements in patient care. As a result, there is an increasing demand for IT professionals in the medical field who can help healthcare organizations harness the power of technology to improve patient outcomes and increase efficiency. Technology has profoundly impacted healthcare, enabling providers to access and share patient information in real-time, perform complex medical procedures with greater precision, and deliver care more efficiently. Electronic health records (EHRs), telemedicine, and other digital health tools have become essential to

94

modern healthcare delivery. IT professionals are crucial in developing, implementing, and maintaining these technologies.

The use of technology in healthcare has also led to a growing need for individuals with specialized IT skills and knowledge, such as data analysis, software development, and cybersecurity. These professionals are tasked with ensuring the security and privacy of patient information, developing innovative solutions to improve patient care, and analyzing large amounts of data to inform decision-making. The following are the IT career opportunities in the medical field:

7.1. **Health Information Manager:** A Health Information Manager (HIM) is a professional responsible for managing the flow of health information within a healthcare organization. They play a critical role in ensuring that patient health information is accurate, secure, and accessible to those who need it. The role of a health information manager includes managing the collection, analysis, and dissemination of patient health information, as well as overseeing the accuracy, security, and privacy of that information. They work closely with healthcare providers, administrators, and other stakeholders to ensure that patient information is used appropriately and to support the delivery of high-quality patient care.

A health information manager's key responsibility is managing the electronic health record (EHR) system. This involves configuring and maintaining the system to ensure it is up-to-date and functioning properly and ensuring the security and privacy of stored patient information. Health information managers also play a critical role in ensuring the accuracy of patient information, working with healthcare providers to resolve discrepancies, and ensuring that the information is complete and up-to-date.

Another essential responsibility of health information managers is to ensure the accessibility of patient information. This includes working with healthcare providers to ensure that they have the appropriate access to patient information and that it is available when and where it is needed. Health information managers may also train healthcare providers to use the EHR and other information technology tools.

Degrees and certifications required: A bachelor's degree in health information management or a related field is usually required for this position. In addition, many HIMs obtain certification from the American Health Information Management Association (AHIMA) as a

Registered Health Information Administrator (RHIA). The RHIA certification is a nationally recognized credential for HIM professionals and demonstrates expertise in managing health information and patient data.

Job growth projections: The demand for HIM professionals is expected to grow as the healthcare industry adopts electronic health records (EHRs) and other health information technology (HIT) systems. According to the Bureau of Labor Statistics, employment of health information managers is projected to grow 11 percent from 2019 to 2029, much faster than the average for all occupations.

Advancement opportunities: Health information managers often have opportunities for advancement within their organizations. They may move into higher-level positions, such as director of health information management or chief privacy officer, or take on additional responsibilities within their current roles.

7.2. **Medical Coder:** A Medical Coder is a professional who assigns codes to diagnoses and procedures to ensure accurate reimbursement for healthcare services. They play a critical role in healthcare by ensuring that medical claims are properly coded and submitted for payment.

The role of a medical coder involves reviewing patient medical records and assigning codes to diagnoses and procedures using standardized classification systems, such as the International Classification of Diseases (ICD) and the Current Procedural Terminology (CPT) codes. Insurance companies and government healthcare programs use these codes to determine the level of reimbursement for healthcare services.

One of the critical responsibilities of a medical coder is to ensure the accuracy of the codes assigned to diagnoses and procedures. This involves thoroughly understanding medical terminology, anatomy, and physiology and the classification systems that assign codes. Medical coders must also stay up-to-date with changes to the classification systems and the codes used to ensure that their coding is accurate and up-to-date.

Another essential responsibility of medical coders is to ensure that medical claims are submitted promptly and accurately. This involves working closely with healthcare providers and billing departments to ensure that the codes assigned to diagnoses and procedures are consistent with the medical record and that the claims are submitted following insurance company and government requirements.

Degrees and certifications required: A high school diploma or equivalent is the minimum education requirement for most medical coding positions. However, some employers may prefer candidates with an associate's degree or certificate in medical coding. Certified Professional Coder (CPC) certification from the American Academy of Professional Coders (AAPC) is widely recognized and highly valued in the medical coding industry.

Job growth projections: The demand for medical coders is expected to grow as the healthcare industry adopts electronic health records (EHRs) and other health information technology (HIT) systems. According to the Bureau of Labor Statistics, employment of medical and health services managers, which includes medical coders, is projected to grow 17 percent from 2019 to 2029, much faster than the average for all occupations.

Advancement opportunities: Medical coders may advance in their careers by moving into supervisory or managerial positions or taking on additional responsibilities within their current roles. Some medical coders specialize in a particular coding area, such as inpatient, outpatient, or anesthesia coding, and can become experts in that area. Some medical coders may pursue additional education and certifications, such as becoming a certified coding specialist or a certified professional coder-physician-based (CPC-P).

7.3. **Health Data Analyst:** A Health Data Analyst is a professional who uses data analytics and visualization tools to support data-driven decision-making in the healthcare industry. They play a critical role in helping healthcare organizations to improve patient care and efficiency by using data to identify trends and patterns and make informed decisions. The role of a health data analyst involves working with large and complex datasets to extract insights and inform decision-making. They use various data analytics and visualization tools to analyze and interpret healthcare data, including patient demographics, medical diagnoses, and treatment outcomes. Health data analysts also work closely with healthcare providers and administrators to understand the questions and problems they are trying to solve and to determine the best way to use data to address these challenges.

One of the critical responsibilities of a health data analyst is to develop and maintain databases and data systems that are used to store and analyze healthcare data. This involves working with healthcare organizations to identify their data needs and designing and implementing data systems that meet them. Health data analysts must also ensure that the data systems they develop are secure and compliant with relevant regulations and standards.

Another essential responsibility of health data analysts is to use data to support decision-making in the healthcare industry. This involves working with healthcare providers and administrators to identify trends and patterns in healthcare data and to use these insights to make informed decisions about patient care, resource allocation, and other critical healthcare issues. Health data analysts may also develop predictive models and algorithms to help healthcare organizations anticipate future needs and respond proactively to changes in the healthcare landscape.

Degrees and certifications required: A bachelor's degree in a related field, such as health informatics, computer science, or statistics, is usually required for health data analyst positions. Some employers may also prefer candidates with a master's degree or certification in health informatics, data analytics, or a related field. In addition, many health data analysts possess certifications in data analytics, such as the Certified Analytics Professional (CAP) certification.

Job growth projections: The demand for health data analysts is expected to grow as healthcare organizations increasingly rely on data to inform decision-making and improve patient outcomes. According to the Bureau of Labor Statistics, employment of medical and health services managers, which include health data analysts, is projected to grow 17 percent from 2019 to 2029, much faster than the average for all occupations.

Advancement opportunities: Health data analysts can advance in their careers by moving into supervisory or managerial positions, taking on additional responsibilities within their current roles, or pursuing advanced education and certifications in data analytics or health informatics. Some health data analysts may choose to specialize in a particular area of healthcare, such as clinical data analysis or public health data analysis. Additionally, some health data analysts may move into related roles, such as health informatics or data science.

7.4. **Clinical Systems Analyst:** A Clinical Systems Analyst is a professional who analyzes, designs, and implements clinical information systems to support patient care. They are critical in helping healthcare organizations improve patient care quality and efficiency by designing and implementing systems that support the clinical workflow and decision-making process. The role of a clinical systems analyst involves working closely with healthcare providers and administrators to understand their needs and to design systems that meet those needs. This may involve analyzing the clinical workflow, identifying opportunities for improvement, and recommending changes to the systems and processes used to support patient care. Clinical systems analysts must also deeply understand healthcare regulations and standards, such as Health Insurance Portability and Accountability Act (HIPAA), to ensure that the systems they design comply with relevant regulations.

One of the critical responsibilities of a clinical systems analyst is to design and implement clinical information systems that support patient care. This involves working with healthcare organizations to determine their specific needs and design systems that meet them. Clinical systems analysts must also understand the technology used to support patient care, including electronic medical record (EMR) systems, clinical decision support systems, and telemedicine systems.

Another essential responsibility of clinical systems analysts is to ensure that the systems they design and implement are user-friendly and meet the needs of the healthcare providers and patients who use them. This involves working with healthcare providers and patients to understand their needs and ensure that the systems are designed and implemented to meet those needs. Clinical systems analysts must also have strong project management skills to ensure that the systems they design and implement are delivered on time and within budget.

Degrees and certifications required: A bachelor's degree in a related field, such as healthcare administration, information technology, or computer science, is typically required for clinical systems analyst positions. Some employers may prefer candidates with a master's degree in a related field, such as healthcare informatics or health administration. Additionally, healthcare information technology or clinical information systems certifications can benefit career advancement.

Job growth projections: The demand for clinical systems analysts is expected to grow as healthcare organizations increasingly adopt technology to improve patient care and support clinical operations. According to the Bureau of Labor Statistics, employment of medical and health services managers, which includes clinical systems analysts, is projected to grow 17 percent from 2019 to 2029, much faster than the average for all occupations.

Advancement opportunities: Clinical systems analysts can advance in their careers by moving into supervisory or managerial positions, taking on additional responsibilities within their current roles, or pursuing advanced education and certifications in healthcare informatics or information technology. Some clinical systems analysts may specialize in a particular area of healthcare technology, such as electronic health records (EHRs) or telemedicine. Additionally, some clinical systems analysts may move into related roles, such as health informatics or healthcare IT project management.

7.5. **Healthcare IT Project Manager:** A Healthcare IT Project Manager is a professional who leads the implementation of IT projects in the healthcare industry and works with cross-functional teams to ensure successful project delivery. They are critical in helping healthcare organizations improve patient care and efficiency by implementing IT projects that support the clinical workflow and decision-making process. The role of a healthcare IT project manager involves working with healthcare

providers and administrators to understand their needs and to design IT projects that meet those needs. This may involve working with clinical systems analysts to analyze the workflow, identify improvement opportunities, and recommend changes to the systems and processes used to support patient care. Healthcare IT project managers must also deeply understand healthcare regulations and standards, such as HIPAA, to ensure that the projects they lead comply with relevant regulations.

One of the critical responsibilities of a healthcare IT project manager is to lead the implementation of IT projects that support patient care. This involves working with cross-functional teams, including clinical systems analysts, healthcare providers, and IT professionals, to ensure that projects are delivered on time, within budget, and to the stakeholders' satisfaction. Healthcare IT project managers must also have strong project management skills to ensure that projects are delivered on time and within budget.

Another essential responsibility of healthcare IT project managers is to ensure that projects are delivered in a way that meets the needs of the stakeholders. This involves working with healthcare providers and administrators to understand their needs and ensure that projects are designed and implemented to meet those needs. Healthcare IT project managers must also have strong communication and interpersonal skills to ensure that they can effectively communicate with stakeholders, resolve conflicts, and build consensus.

Degrees and certifications required: A bachelor's degree in a relevant field, such as healthcare administration, information technology, or computer science, is typically needed in the profession. Professional certifications, such as the Project Management Professional (PMP) certification, can also help advance in this career field.

Job growth projections: According to the Bureau of Labor Statistics (BLS), the employment of healthcare IT project managers is expected to grow 11% from 2019 to 2029, faster than the average for all occupations. This growth is due to the increasing adoption of technology in the healthcare industry and the need for IT professionals who can manage and oversee IT projects.

Advancement opportunities: Healthcare IT project managers can advance in their careers by taking on increasingly complex and high-level IT projects and obtaining advanced degrees or certifications. Some healthcare IT project managers may also move into higher-level management positions, such as IT directors or CIOs.

7.6. **Telemedicine Systems Analyst:** A Telemedicine Systems Analyst specializes in designing and implementing telemedicine systems to support remote patient care. They play a critical role in the rapidly growing field of telemedicine by helping healthcare organizations to provide quality care to patients from remote locations. The role of a telemedicine systems analyst involves working with healthcare providers and administrators to understand their needs for remote patient care and to design telemedicine systems that meet those needs. This may include working with healthcare IT project managers to identify the best telemedicine technology, working with clinical systems analysts to integrate telemedicine systems into the clinical workflow, and working with healthcare providers to ensure that telemedicine systems are used effectively.

One of the critical responsibilities of a telemedicine systems analyst is to design and implement telemedicine systems that support remote patient care. This involves selecting the best telemedicine technology, working with clinical systems analysts to integrate telemedicine systems into the clinical workflow, and working with healthcare providers to ensure that telemedicine systems are used effectively. Telemedicine systems analysts must also deeply understand telemedicine regulations and standards, such as HIPAA, to ensure that the systems they design and implement comply with relevant regulations.

Another essential responsibility of telemedicine systems analysts is to ensure that telemedicine systems are user-friendly and accessible to healthcare providers and patients. This involves working with healthcare providers and administrators to understand their needs for telemedicine systems and to design systems that meet those needs. Telemedicine systems analysts must also have strong communication and interpersonal skills to ensure that they can effectively communicate with stakeholders, resolve conflicts, and build consensus.

Degrees and Certifications Required: To become a Telemedicine Systems Analyst, you typically need a bachelor's degree in a related field, such as computer science, information technology, or healthcare management. Relevant certifications, such as those offered by the Healthcare Information and Management Systems Society (HIMSS), can enhance your career opportunities.

Job Growth Projections: The demand for telemedicine systems analysts is growing as the healthcare industry increasingly relies on technology to support remote patient care. The U.S. Bureau of Labor Statistics projects that employment in the healthcare and IT industries will grow much faster than the average for all occupations in the coming years, providing ample opportunities for telemedicine systems analysts.

Advancement Opportunities: As a Telemedicine Systems Analyst, you may start your career as a junior analyst and work your way up to a senior analyst or project manager role. You can also consider specializing in a specific aspect of telemedicine, such as telehealth software development or telehealth network security, and become a subject matter expert. Additionally, you can pursue advanced degrees in relevant fields to further your career advancement.

7.7. **Medical Device Software Developer:** A Medical Device Software Developer is a professional who specializes in designing and developing software for medical devices. They play a critical role in the healthcare industry by helping to create innovative and effective medical devices that improve patient care. The role of a medical device software developer involves working with healthcare organizations, medical device manufacturers, and researchers to understand their needs for medical devices and to design software that meets those needs. This

may involve working with other IT professionals, such as clinical systems analysts, health data analysts, and telemedicine systems analysts, to ensure that the software is integrated with other healthcare systems and supports patient care.

One of the critical responsibilities of a medical device software developer is to design and develop software for medical devices that meets the needs of healthcare organizations and patients. This involves working with healthcare organizations, medical device manufacturers, and researchers to understand their medical device needs and design software that meets them. Software developers must also understand medical device regulations and standards, such as the U.S. Food and Drug Administration. (FDA's) regulations to ensure that the software they develop is compliant with relevant regulations.

Another essential responsibility of medical device software developers is to ensure that medical device software is user-friendly and accessible to healthcare providers and patients. This involves working with healthcare providers and administrators to understand their medical device software needs and design software that meets those needs. Medical device software developers must also have strong communication and interpersonal skills to ensure that they can effectively communicate with stakeholders, resolve conflicts, and build consensus.

Degrees and Certifications Required: Medical device software developers typically have a degree in computer science, software engineering, or a related field. Some employers may also require a master's degree. Relevant certifications, such as those offered by the Institute for the Certification of Healthcare IT Professionals (ICHITP) or the Healthcare Information and Management Systems Society (HIMSS), can also increase a candidate's chances of employment and advancement.

Job Growth Projections: According to the Bureau of Labor Statistics (BLS), computer and information technology employment is projected to grow 11% from 2019 to 2029, much faster than the average for all occupations. The demand for medical device software developers is expected to increase as the use of technology in the healthcare industry continues to grow.

Advancement Opportunities: Medical device software developers can advance their careers by taking on leadership roles like project managers or directors. They can also specialize in a particular area of medical device software development, such as developing software for medical devices used in the operating room or for managing patient data. Pursuing further education, such as a master's degree, and obtaining additional certifications can also increase advancement opportunities.

7.8. Electronic Health Record (EHR)

Administrator: An Electronic Health Record (EHR) Administrator specializes in configuring, maintaining, and supporting electronic health record (EHR) systems. They play a critical role in the healthcare industry by ensuring that EHR systems are secure, accurate, and accessible to healthcare providers and patients. The role of an EHR administrator involves working with healthcare organizations, providers, and IT professionals to understand their needs for EHR systems and configure EHR systems that meet those needs. This may include working with other IT professionals, such as clinical systems analysts, health data analysts, and telemedicine systems analysts, to ensure that the EHR system is integrated with other healthcare systems and supports patient care.

One of the critical responsibilities of an EHR administrator is to configure, maintain, and support EHR systems to ensure data accuracy and security. This involves working with healthcare organizations, healthcare providers, and IT professionals to understand their needs for EHR systems and to configure EHR systems that meet those needs. EHR administrators must also deeply understand EHR regulations and standards, such as the HIPAA EHR regulations, to ensure that the EHR systems they administer comply with relevant regulations.

Another essential responsibility of EHR administrators is to ensure that EHR systems are user-friendly and accessible to healthcare providers and patients. This involves working with healthcare providers and administrators to understand their needs for EHR systems and to configure EHR systems that meet those needs. EHR administrators must also have strong communication and interpersonal skills to ensure that they can effectively communicate with stakeholders, resolve conflicts, and build consensus.

Degrees and Certifications Required: A bachelor's degree in health informatics, computer science, or a related field is typically required for an EHR Administrator position. Some employers may also prefer a master's degree. In addition, certifications such as Certified Professional in Health Information Technology (CPHIT), Certified Electronic Health Records Specialist (CEHRS), and Healthcare Information and Management Systems Society (HIMSS) are also highly valued.

Job Growth Projections: According to the Bureau of Labor Statistics (BLS), employment of medical and health services managers, including EHR Administrators, is projected to grow 18% from 2019 to 2029, much faster than the average for all occupations. The growth in the healthcare industry, particularly in the use of electronic health records, is driving the demand for EHR Administrators.

Advancement Opportunities: EHR Administrators can advance to higher-level positions in health information management, such as health information technology director, health information management director, or chief medical information officer. They can also move into related positions such as clinical systems analyst, healthcare IT project manager, or health data analyst. Continued education and professional development are essential for advancement opportunities in this field.

7.9. **Bioinformatics Analyst:** A Bioinformatics Analyst is a professional specializing in applying computer science and information technology to analyze biological data. They play a critical role in healthcare by using their technical skills to support medical research and drug discovery. The role of a bioinformatics analyst involves

working with biological researchers and healthcare organizations to understand their needs for data analysis and to design and implement data analysis solutions that meet those needs. This may involve working with other IT professionals: such as health data analysts, to ensure they are integrated with other healthcare systems and support patient care.

One of the critical responsibilities of a bioinformatics analyst is to apply computer science and information technology to analyze biological data. This involves designing and implementing data analysis solutions optimized for specific types of biological data, such as genomics, proteomics, or metabolomics. Bioinformatics analysts must also deeply understand algorithms and techniques, such as sequence alignment, gene expression analysis, and pathway analysis, to ensure their data analysis solutions are accurate and effective.

Another essential responsibility of bioinformatics analysts is communicating their findings to biological researchers and healthcare organizations. This involves working with biological researchers and healthcare organizations to understand their needs for data analysis and to communicate the results of their data analysis in a meaningful and actionable way. Bioinformatics analysts must also have strong communication and interpersonal skills to ensure that they can effectively communicate with stakeholders, resolve conflicts, and build consensus.

Degrees and certifications required: A bachelor's or master's degree in bioinformatics, computer science, biology, or a related field is required for entry-level positions in bioinformatics. Additionally, certifications in specific software or technologies can also be beneficial.

Job growth projections: The demand for bioinformatics analysts is expected to grow rapidly in the coming years due to the increasing use of technology in medical research and drug discovery. According to the Bureau of Labor Statistics, employment of computer and information research scientists, which includes bioinformatics analysts, is projected to grow 11 percent from 2019 to 2029.

Advancement opportunities: With experience, bioinformatics analysts can advance to senior positions such as lead bioinformatics analyst, bioinformatics manager, or bioinformatics director. In these roles, they may have more responsibilities and have the opportunity to lead research projects and manage teams. Additionally, some bioinformatics analysts may pursue further education and become researchers or scientists in the field of bioinformatics.

7.10. **Health IT Security Specialist:** A Health IT Security Specialist ensures the security and privacy of electronic health information in the healthcare industry. They play a critical role in protecting against cyber threats and data breaches, which can seriously affect patients and healthcare organizations. The role of a health IT security specialist involves working with healthcare organizations to understand their security and privacy needs and to design and implement security solutions that meet those needs. This may include working with other IT professionals, such as clinical systems analysts and EHR administrators, to ensure that the security solutions are integrated with other healthcare systems and support patient care.

One of the critical responsibilities of a health IT security specialist is to ensure the security and privacy of electronic health information. This involves designing and implementing security solutions optimized for healthcare organizations' specific types of electronic health information, such as electronic health records (EHRs), telemedicine systems, and medical devices. Health IT security specialists must also understand security and privacy regulations, such as HIPAA, to ensure their security solutions comply with applicable laws and regulations.

Another essential responsibility of health IT security specialists is to protect against cyber threats and data breaches. This involves working with healthcare organizations to understand their potential threats and implement security solutions that can prevent or detect those threats. Health IT security specialists must also have a deep understanding of cybersecurity technologies and techniques, such as firewalls, intrusion detection systems, and encryption, to ensure that the security solutions they implement are effective.

Degrees and certifications required: A bachelor's degree in computer science, information technology, cybersecurity, or a related field is required for the career. Certifications such as Certified Information Systems Security Professional (CISSP) and Certified Ethical Hacker (CEH) can demonstrate expertise in the field and boost career advancement opportunities.

Job growth projections: The demand for health IT security specialists are growing as the healthcare industry increasingly relies on technology. According to the Bureau of Labor Statistics (BLS), employment of information security analysts is projected to grow 32% from 2019 to 2029, much faster than the average for all occupations.

Advancement opportunities: With experience, a health IT security specialist can advance to a leadership role, such as chief information security officer or director of security operations. Health IT security specialists can also specialize in a particular area of healthcare technology security, such as mobile device security or cloud security. Continuing education and professional development opportunities can also enhance career advancement opportunities in this field.

Conclusion

The medical field provides various IT career opportunities, such as Health Information Manager, Medical Coder, Health Data Analyst, Clinical Systems Analyst, Healthcare IT Project Manager, Telemedicine Systems Analyst, Medical Device Software Developer, Electronic Health Record (EHR) Administrator, Bioinformatics Analyst, and Health IT Security Specialist. Each position has unique responsibilities and requires specific skills and knowledge to perform. For example, a Health Information Manager is responsible for managing the flow of health information and ensuring its accuracy, security, and accessibility, while a Medical Device Software Developer designs and develops software for medical devices. These careers offer a range of challenges and opportunities to those interested in IT and healthcare.

Chapter EIGHT

Questions and Answers for Interviews

Introduction to interview questions

An interview is a conversation between a job candidate and an employer, during which the employer assesses the candidate's suitability for a position. The employer uses interview questions to gather information about the candidate's skills, experiences, and qualifications. Interview questions can be divided into several categories, including behavioral, technical, motivational, and situational. It is essential for the candidate to be prepared for a range of interview questions and to answer them clearly and concisely. It is also necessary for the candidate to ask questions during the interview, as this shows their interest in the company and the position.

8.1. General Interview Questions and Answers (Samples)

Interviewer: "Tell me about yourself."

Candidate: "I am a recent graduate with a degree in computer science. During college, I gained experience through internships at tech companies, where I worked on software development and data analysis projects. I enjoy staying updated on the latest technologies and participating in coding competitions in my free time. I am excited to apply my skills and knowledge professionally and am looking for a company where I can grow and develop as a software engineer."

Interviewer: "Tell me a little about yourself and your background."

Candidate: "Sure. My name names], and I am currently pursuing a degree in [Field of Study] at [University]. I have gained relevant experience through internships at company] and company], where I worked on projects related to [Skill/Task]. In my most recent internship, I developed strong [Skill/Task] skills and gained valuable experience working with a team. I am excited to apply these skills and experiences to a full-time role."

Interviewer: "What attracted you to this company?"

Candidate: "I was attracted to this company because of its reputation as a leader in the tech industry and its commitment to innovation. I believe that this company's values and culture align with my own and that I would thrive in this environment. I am also impressed by the opportunities for growth and professional development this company offers, and I am excited about working on challenging and meaningful projects."

Interviewer: "Why are you interested in this position?"

Candidate: "I am interested in this position because the company] is a leader in the industry] industry, and I am excited to contribute to the company's success. My skills and experiences make me a strong fit for this role, and I am eager to learn and grow with the company. I am particularly interested in the opportunity to work on

[Project/Task] and believe that my skills and experiences make me well-suited for this type of work."

Interviewer: "What are your strengths?"

Candidate: "My strengths include my strong analytical and problem-solving skills, ability to work well in a team, and attention to detail. I am also proactive and self-motivated and enjoy taking on new challenges and learning new technologies."

Candidate: "My biggest strength is working well in a team. I have a strong track record of collaborating with others and contributing to the success of group projects. I am also a quick learner and always look for ways to improve and expand my skills. In my previous internships, I have received positive feedback for my attention to detail and ability to meet deadlines."

Interviewer: "What are your weaknesses?"

Candidate: "One of my weaknesses is that I sometimes get too involved in my work and may need to remind myself to take breaks and prioritize my work-life balance. I am actively working on managing my time more effectively and delegating tasks when necessary. Another weakness is that I can be a perfectionist sometimes and may need to remind myself to let go of the need for perfection to meet deadlines and stay focused on the bigger picture."

Interviewer: "Why should we hire you?"

Candidate: "I am the best candidate for this position because I combine technical skills, relevant experience, and personal qualities. My technical skills, as demonstrated through my degree in computer science and my internships in the tech industry, make me well-equipped to handle the responsibilities of this position. My experience working on collaborative projects and strong communication skills make me an asset to any team. I am also highly motivated and committed to achieving success in my career, and I am eager to contribute my skills and knowledge to the success of this company."

8.2. Behavioral Interview Questions and Answers (Samples)

Behavioral questions are common interview questions that ask candidates to describe specific situations they have encountered and how they dealt with them. These questions assess the candidate's problem-solving skills and ability to handle challenges. Here are some examples of behavioral questions and sample answers:

Interviewer: "Tell me about a time when you had to work with a difficult team member. How did you handle the situation?"

Candidate: "I once had to work with a consistently negative team member who was resistant to new ideas. Rather than getting frustrated, I tried to understand their perspective and see if any underlying issues might be causing their behavior. I also tried regularly communicating with them and including them in decision-making processes. As a result, we could find common ground and work together effectively."

Interviewer: "Describe when you had to handle a high-pressure situation. How did you stay calm under pressure?"

Candidate: "I once had to lead a project with a tight deadline and many moving parts. I broke the project into smaller tasks to stay calm under pressure and delegated responsibilities to team members. I also kept clear and regular communication with my team and prioritized the most important tasks first. We completed the project on time and to a high standard by staying organized and focused."

Interviewer: "Tell me about a time when you had to make a difficult decision. How did you go about making the decision?"

Candidate: "I once had to decide whether to accept a job offer or turn it down. To make the decision, I weighed the pros and cons of each option and considered how each would impact my long-term career goals. I also sought the advice of trusted mentors and colleagues. In the end, I made the decision that I believed would be the best fit for me and my career."

8.3. Technical Interview Questions and Answers (Samples)

Technical interview questions are common questions specific to a particular field or industry and are used to assess the candidate's knowledge and skills. Here are some examples of technical interview questions and sample answers:

Interviewer: "How do you handle debugging in [Programming Language]?"

Candidate: "When debugging in [Programming Language], I typically use a combination of print statements and debugging tools, such as the debugger built into the

[Programming Language] development environment. I also try to isolate the problem by commenting out sections of code and testing to see which section is causing the issue. If necessary, I will consult the documentation or seek the help of more experienced colleagues."

Interviewer: "What is the difference between a stack and a queue?"

Candidate "A stack is a data structure that allows for inserting and removing elements only at the top of the stack. This is known as a last-in, first-out (LIFO) structure. On the other hand, a queue is a first-in, first-out (FIFO) structure, where elements are added at the back of the queue and removed from the front. Stacks are often used for tasks such as reversing the order of elements, while queues are used for tasks such as scheduling."

Interviewer: "How would you implement [Algorithm] in [Programming Language]?"

Candidate: "To implement an Algorithm in Programming Language, I would follow these steps: [Step 1], [Step 2], [Step 3], etc. It is important to ensure that the algorithm is optimized for performance and that proper error handling is implemented. I would also consider using any built-in libraries or functions that might make the implementation simpler and more efficient."

8.4. Motivational Interview Questions and Answers (Samples)

Motivational interview questions are common questions that ask candidates about their career goals and what motivates them. These questions assess the candidate's fit with the company culture and long-term career aspirations. Here are some examples of motivational interview questions and sample answers:

Interviewer: "What are your long-term career goals?"
Candidate: "My long-term career goal is to become a leader in my field and positively impact my organization. I am motivated by the opportunity to take on new challenges and contribute my skills and expertise to the team. I am also excited about the possibility of continuing to learn and grow as a professional."

Interviewer: "What motivates you in your career?"
Candidate: "I am motivated by the opportunity to make a difference and positively impact the world. I am also motivated by chance to learn and grow professionally and

take on new challenges and responsibilities. I enjoy working in a collaborative and dynamic environment where I can contribute my skills and ideas and be part of a team working towards a common goal."

Interviewer: "What are you looking for in your next job?"

Candidate: "In my next job, I am looking for the opportunity to make a meaningful contribution to the organization and work with a team of passionate professionals. I am also looking for the opportunity to learn and grow professionally and take on new challenges and responsibilities. I believe positive company culture is important, and I am looking for an organization that values diversity, collaboration, and innovation."

8.5. Situational Interview Questions and Answers (Samples)

Situational interview questions are common questions that ask the candidate to describe how they would handle a hypothetical situation. These questions assess the candidate's decision-making skills and ability to think independently. Here are some examples of situational interview questions and sample answers:

Interviewer: "Tell me about a time when you had to make a quick decision under pressure. How did you handle the situation?"

Candidate: "I once had to make a quick decision under pressure when working as a [Job Title] at the company]. We were in the middle of a [Task], and one of our key pieces of equipment broke down. I knew we had a tight deadline and needed to find a solution quickly. I assessed the situation and determined that the best course of action was to action]. I communicated my decision to the team, and we could complete the task on time. Looking back, I learned the importance of staying calm under pressure and having a clear action plan."

Interviewer: "Describe when you had to deal with a conflict at work. How did you resolve the situation?"

Candidate: "I once had to deal with a conflict when working as a [Job Title] at the company]. Two team members disagreed about how to approach a [Task]. Rather than letting the conflict escalate, I facilitated a meeting between the team members to discuss the issue. I listened to both sides and helped them reach a mutually comfortable compromise. By addressing the conflict head-on and finding a resolution, we could move forward and complete the task successfully."

Interviewer: "Tell me about a time when you had to persuade someone to see your point of view. How did you handle the situation?"

Candidate: "I once had to persuade someone to see my point of view when I was working as a [Job Title] at the company]. One of my colleagues was resistant to a new approach that I thought would be more effective for a [Task]. I knew it was essential to convince them, as our success depended on it. To persuade them, I presented them with data and research that supported my point of view, and I also listened to their concerns and addressed them. Ultimately, they were convinced, and we successfully implemented the new approach.

8.6.   Questions to Ask the Interviewer

(Samples)

Remember to tailor your questions based on the role you're interviewing for, the company, and the conversation you've had so far. Asking thoughtful questions not only helps you gather valuable information about the company, but also shows your genuine interest and enthusiasm for the job.

Candidate: "Can you tell me more about the company culture and values?"

Candidate: "What qualities do you think are most important for success in this role?"

Candidate: "What is a typical day like for someone in this role?"

Candidate: "What qualities do you think are most important for success in this role?:

Candidate: "What are some of the biggest challenges that someone in this role might face?"

Candidate: "How does the company measure success in this role?"

8.7. Passing Your Virtual Job Interview

Tip #1: *Test your technology beforehand.*

Before your virtual interview, test your internet connection, microphone, and webcam. You want to ensure that the technical aspects of your interview go smoothly and that you can be seen and heard clearly. It can also be helpful to have a backup plan in case of any technical issues, such as having a phone nearby that you can use to call into the interview.

Tip #2: *Dress appropriately.*

Even though the interview is virtual, you should still dress as you would for an in-person interview. Avoid wearing loud patterns or bright colors, as they can be distracting on camera. This shows that you are taking the interview seriously and professionally.

Tip #3: *Set up a professional-looking background.*
Avoid having clutter or personal items visible in the frame. Choose a background that is neat and does not have any distractions. If you have a plain wall, that can be a good option. If not, consider using a virtual background.

Tip #4: *Practice active listening and make eye contact.*
In a virtual interview, getting distracted or losing focus can be easy. Pay attention to the interviewer and show that you are listening by nodding and asking follow-up questions. To create the illusion of eye contact, look directly at the webcam.

Tip #5: *Show enthusiasm and passion for the job.*
Let your passion and enthusiasm for the job shine through in your answers. Be sure to research the company beforehand and be prepared to discuss why you are interested in the role and how you can contribute to the company's success.

Conclusion

The future of work is constantly evolving and presents challenges and opportunities for individuals and businesses.

The rapid pace of technological change and increasing global competition are transforming the nature of work, leading to the "rise of new roles and the decline of others" (World Economic Forum, 2020). This changing landscape presents both challenges and opportunities for individuals and businesses. According to the McKinsey Global Institute, the proliferation of artificial intelligence and automation will lead to both the displacement of some jobs and the creation of new ones (2017). It is, therefore, crucial for individuals to anticipate the potential impact of these technologies on their industry and to proactively seek out opportunities to upskill and stay competitive. At the same time, the future of work also presents opportunities for individuals and businesses to innovate and adapt. The World Economic Forum's "The Future of Jobs Report 2020" suggests that the changing nature of work presents an opportunity for individuals to "actively seek out opportunities to learn, network, and stay current" to stay competitive in the job market (2020). It also presents an opportunity for businesses to adapt to changing market dynamics and find new ways to create value.

By Staying Informed and Proactive, Individuals can Position themselves for Success in Emerging Careers

In a rapidly changing job market, staying current on the latest developments in your field and anticipating these changes' impact on your industry. The McKinsey Global Institute advises individuals to "invest in lifelong learning" to stay current and adapt to the changing nature of work (2017). This may involve pursuing additional education, such as a degree or certification, or ongoing professional development to update your skills. It is also essential to be proactive in seeking opportunities to gain experience in your field. The Fast Company article "How to Pivot into an Emerging Career" suggests internships, entry-level positions, and volunteer work as ways to gain experience and build your skillset (2016). The World Economic Forum's "The Future of Jobs Report 2020" suggests that individuals should "actively seek out opportunities to learn, network, and stay current" to stay competitive in the job market (2020). By staying informed and proactive, you can position yourself for success in an increasingly competitive job market.

FURTHER READING

Accenture. "The Future of Fintech and Banking: Digitally Disruptive." https://www.accenture.com/us-en/insights/fintech/future-of-fintech

American Health Information Management Association. (n.d.). What is Health Information Management? Retrieved from https://www.ahima.org/careers/what-is-him

American Medical Informatics Association (AMIA). (n.d.). What is Clinical Informatics? Retrieved February 10, 2023, from https://www.amia.org/what-clinical-informatics

Bureau of Labor Statistics, US Department of Labor, Occupational Outlook Handbook, Human Resources Managers, at https://www.bls.gov/ooh/management/human-resources-managers.htm (visited January 06, 2023).

Bureau of Labor Statistics. (2021, March 31). Medical and Health Services Managers. Occupational Outlook Handbook. Retrieved from https://www.bls.gov/ooh/management/medical-and-health-services-managers.htm

Bureau of Labor Statistics. (2021, April). Occupational Outlook Handbook: Medical and Health Services Managers. Retrieved February 10, 2023, from https://www.bls.gov/ooh/management/medical-and-health-services-managers.htm

Centers for Disease Control and Prevention (CDC). (2021). Health IT Workforce. Retrieved February 10, 2023, from https://www.cdc.gov/healthit/healthit-workforce/index.html.

Congressional Research Service. (2018). The Future of Work: Robots, AI, and Automation.

Deloitte. "Banking on Fintech: A strategic partnership."
https://www2.deloitte.com/us/en/insights/industry/fin
ancial-services/banking-on-fintech-a-strategic-
partnership.html.

European Union's Digital Single Market Team. (2019).
The Future of Work in the Digital Economy.

Fast Company. (2016). How to Pivot into an Emerging
Career.

Forbes. (2018). The Most Common Job Interview
Questions and How to Answer Them.

Forbes. (2019). Emerging Careers in the Digital Age.

Forbes. (2020). How to Ace Your Virtual Job Interview.

Glassdoor. (2021). Phone Interview Questions and
Answers.

Glassdoor. (2021). Common Interview Questions and
Answers.

Glassdoor. (2021). Behavioral Interview Questions and
Answers.

Glassdoor. (2021). Virtual Interview Tips.

Glassdoor. (2021). Technical Interview Questions and
Answers.

Harvard Business Review. (2018). Navigating the Future of
Work.

Health IT Careers. (n.d.). Health Data Analyst. Retrieved
from https://healthitcareers.com/health-data-analyst/

Healthcare Information and Management Systems Society.
(n.d.). Clinical Systems Analyst. Retrieved from
https://www.himss.org/clinical-systems-analyst

HealthIT.gov. (2021). What is Health IT? Retrieved
February 10, 2023, from
https://www.healthit.gov/topic/health-it-basics/what-
health-it.

IIBA (2019). Business Analysis in the Technology
Industry. https://www.iiba.org/industry-
resources/business-analysis-in-the-technology-
industry/.

Indeed. (2019). Technical Interview Questions and Answers.

International Labour Organization. (2019). The Future of Work: Employment, Skills and Workforce Strategy for the Fourth Industrial Revolution.

Li, Y., Li, X., Li, X., & Su, X. (2019). Wearable sensors in healthcare. Frontiers of information technology & electronic engineering, 20(8), 727-737.

McKinsey Global Institute. (2017). Preparing for the Future of Work.

National Institute of Standards and Technology (NIST). (2020). Health IT Security. Retrieved February 10, 2023, from https://www.nist.gov/itl/applied-cybersecurity/healthcare/health-it-security.

Organization for Economic Co-operation and Development (OECD). (2017). Preparing for the Future of Work in the Digital Age.

Oxford Martin School. (2014). Rise of the Machines: The Future of Jobs in the Age of Automation.

Patel, V., & Jain, N. (2017). Benefits and challenges of electronic health records. Journal of medical systems, 41(12), 375.

PMI (2020). Project Management Job Growth and Talent Gap 2017-2027. https://www.pmi.org/-/media/pmi/documents/public/pdf/learning/talent-gap-report.pdf.

PwC. "Global FinTech report 2019: Embracing disruption." https://www.pwc.com/gx/en/financial-services/fintech/pwc-fintech-survey-2019.html.

The Muse. (2019). The 30 Best Questions to Ask in an Interview (And How to Answer Them).

The Muse. (2020). How to Ace Your Virtual Job Interview (Because Yes, It's Different).

Topol, E. J. (2019). High-performance medicine: the convergence of human and artificial intelligence. Nature Medicine, 25(1), 44-56.

Wang, S., & Kaushal, R. (2019). Telemedicine and e-health: past, present, and future. Journal of medical systems, 43(6), 398.

World Bank. (2015). The Future of Jobs: The Future of Work in the 21st century.

World Economic Forum. (2020). The Future of Jobs Report 2020.